DON'T CALL ME BACK

Urban Trauma

The journey continues

LT4LIFE

Andre Hart Sr.

Baltimore Md.

Table of Contents

"Sometimes the hardest roads lead to the most beautiful destinations. But first, you must walk through the pain."

Dedication

To my family, I love you more than anything. And to every single person who supported me during the journey of writing my first book and after its publication, *I Found a Way Out*—thank you, thank you, thank you. Your encouragement was not just uplifting; it gave me the strength and clarity to write this next chapter, *Don't Call Me Back*. Your belief in me opened my heart with compassion, expanded my thinking, and gave me the emotional courage to look back—honestly. To face the truth behind the choices I made. This book is rooted in that truth. It is a reflection on trauma, on survival, and on the decisions so many young adults make while living with the weight of urban trauma. Thank you for helping me find my way through it. Again.

With love and gratitude,

Andre Hart Sr.

Introduction
Why "Don't Call Me Back" Matters

A Love Letter to Who I Was. A Boundary for Who I Am.

Don't call me back—not with your voice and not with your assumptions. Don't call me back with the memory of who I had to be just to survive where I came from. Don't call me back with the labels the system placed on me: "disruptive," "difficult," and "dangerous." You saw the anger but not the cause. You noticed the scars but never asked about the story behind them. Don't call me back to the streets that raised me hard. Where gunshots replaced lullabies and sirens came before the sun rose. Where "make it home" wasn't something you said lightly—it was a prayer. Where joy felt like a setup, and trust could cost your life. Don't call me back to the silence, the kind that hums in underfunded schools, over-crowded housing, and the ache of being overlooked. Don't call me back to the cold that came not just from the weather but from a world that never saw us as children, only suspects. And don't call me back by the name Jim Hart if all you want is to see whether the trauma still fits or if I have any reservations about returning to the old me. That version of me was built by survival and forged in a system that punishes pain where he couldn't show emotions and taught boys like me to fight or be forgotten. He was armor. A way to stay alive in a world that punished pain and mocked vulnerability. He was necessary back then, but I am no longer living in that war zone. I've moved on. Not just physically but emotionally, spiritually, and systemically. I have changed in the core of who I am. When trauma is handed down like a family name, healing doesn't happen by accident. You have to fight for it. You have to unlearn, feel, and believe that you deserve more than just getting by. People look at me now and think I'm soft because I'm calm. But this calm isn't a weakness—it's a strength. My peace isn't something I stumbled into. It's something I built, piece by piece, breath by breath, after years of not knowing what peace even felt like. It's not performative. It's not temporary. It's discipline. It's a boundary. It's knowing when to walk away and when to protect what you've worked hard to build.

So, when I say, "don't call me back," I'm not denying my past. I'm just choosing to protect my present. I'm drawing a clear line between who I was and who I am now. Between survival and healing. This is a message to everyone who's had to grow up too fast. To the boys who were told to toughen up before they were even old enough to know what they were feeling. To the girls who became caretakers while they were still figuring out who they were. To anyone who had to learn how to stay alive in places where dreams were caged, and futures were fenced in. Don't call me back to the version of me that lived in fear. That confused numbness for strength. That wore pain like a uniform. I've outgrown that life. I define who I am now—not the system, not the street, not the pain. I am not pretending my past didn't happen. I'm just refusing to let it control me anymore. I am honoring where I came from by refusing to stay stuck there. Moving forward means carrying your history with compassion, not chains. It means saying, "Yes, I was that—but I am also this."

So, no. Don't call me back.

Not to the pain.

Not to the performance.

Not to the prison of who I had to be.

Chapter One
The Cost of Becoming Me

A Story of Survival

This story isn't just about making it out alive; it's about what it costs to *stay* alive when everything around you is designed to kill your hope, your identity, and your sense of self. It's about what it means to wake up every day in a war zone that doesn't wear uniforms or fly flags but still leaves bodies on the pavement and spirits buried under silence. It's about surviving a war that no one calls a war, fought on your blocks, in your classrooms, in your home, and most of all, in your mind.

In my first book, *I Found a Way Out*, I told the story of how I escaped the streets. But what I've come to understand is that leaving the streets physically was only half the battle. The harder part came later—when I realized that the streets were still living *in me*. They had shaped how I saw myself. How I loved. How I reacted. How I defended and destroyed myself at the same time. I had spent years fighting to survive, but I never stopped to ask: *What kind of man am I becoming just to stay alive?* Survival gave me armor, but it also gave me numbness. It taught me how to shut down instead of open up. How to keep moving instead of feeling. How to win fights but lose relationships. How to be feared but never fully known. That's the residue no one talks about. The residue that survival leaves behind. It doesn't show up in medical records or mugshots. It lives in how you flinch at softness. How you trust no one. How you sleep with one eye open even when you're safe. It lives in the silence after the violence, in the memories that replay like broken records, in the grief you never gave yourself permission to feel.

Healing—real healing—demanded more than just distance from the block. It demanded *honesty*. Brutal honesty. The kind that made me sit with everything I had run from. It demanded *courage*, not the kind you need to face an enemy, but the kind you need to face your *own reflection*. It demanded that I stop presenting strength and start practicing vulnerability. It demanded daily self-discipline, exhaustion, and often loneliness of making a choice to choose a different way. A way that didn't come naturally. A way that didn't promise quick results. A way that required me to unlearn everything I once believed made me strong. Because strength isn't how much you can carry; sometimes, strength is how much you're willing to *put* down so you can finally breathe. So no, this story isn't just about how I made it out; it's about how I learned to come back to myself. To rebuild a man I never thought I could be. To choose healing again and again, even when it hurts. That's what it means to go beyond survival.

A Place Built to Contain Us

When I reflect on my experience of living in Lexington Terrace, it wasn't just a neighborhood, it was a cage. And I wasn't just a resident. I was someone who had been *placed* there, locked in a system that didn't see me as a person worthy of freedom or possibility. Lexington Terrace was born from cold, calculated decisions made far away from the voices of the people who lived there. In 1958, Baltimore's Lexington Terrace public housing opened as "Negro housing," with 99% of its residents being Black, reflecting a broader pattern of racially segregated public housing in the city, including developments like Poe Homes (Wright, 2018).

A label that wasn't just a name, "Negro housing," it was a sentence. A sentence that said, *you don't belong anywhere else. You will be confined here, out of sight, out of mind.* It was a physical and symbolic marker of segregation—a place designed not to nurture or empower but to isolate and contain. The walls weren't just concrete and brick—they were barriers, invisible lines drawn by history, policy, and prejudice. The city didn't just build housing; it built a prison without bars, a world that whispered every day, *this is all you get.* We weren't supposed to dream here. We weren't supposed to grow or escape or hope. We were supposed to stay in these concrete hallways with broken elevators, generation after generation, carrying the weight of neglect like a shroud. Neglect was everywhere. The buildings rotted, and the playgrounds, once meant for laughter, were haunted by silence and danger. No new paint, no fresh investments, no second chances. The way hope felt like a luxury no one around us could afford. The way every day was a battle just to believe you mattered.

But here's the cruelest part: for many of us, that cage was dressed up as "home." And so we lived inside the walls of what was supposed to protect us but too often felt like it was suffocating us. We learned early that freedom was something other people had. And if we wanted to survive, we had to bury those dreams deep inside. It's a strange kind of pain to grow up knowing you're loved but also knowing the world doesn't want to love your back. To be hugged by family and crushed by circumstance. To fight for air in a space that seems determined to keep you underwater. Every cracked window and faded stairwell told a story of broken promises. Every siren in the night was a reminder that safety was never guaranteed. Every friend lost, every gunshot fired, every mother's tears—all echoes of a place built to contain us but never to set us free.

And yet, despite it all, we fought. We found moments of joy, of laughter, of brotherhood. We held onto scraps of hope like they were lifelines. Because even inside a cage, the human spirit can refuse to be caged. But the scars run deep. The pain isn't just in the buildings or the streets. It's in the way you see yourself after living in a place that was never meant to hold your dreams. It shapes your fears, your choices, and your self-worth. It haunts the silent moments when you wonder if you're really free or just free to survive another day. This place was more than a home. It was a statement. A warning. A wound. And living in Lexington Terrace meant carrying that wound—on your back, in your heart, and beneath your skin—for as long as you lived.

Segregation by Design

The trauma of Lexington Terrace didn't just happen. It was built brick by brick, policy by policy. It was no accident. It was designed. For generations, our community was systematically denied access to the very foundations of a decent life: good schools, safe streets, clean air, economic opportunity, and basic respect. What other neighborhoods took for granted, we were taught to accept as impossible dreams. They redlined us—drawing invisible lines on maps that dictated who deserved investment and who was destined for neglect. They ignored us—turning a blind eye to crumbling buildings, failing schools, and mounting despair. They criminalized us—casting suspicion on Black youth before they even had a chance to prove themselves. The city starved us. Starved us of resources, hope, and dignity. And then, when we struggled to survive when hunger and pain pushed us to the edge, they blamed *us* for being hungry. Our pain was labeled pathology. Our grief was dismissed as dysfunction. With our survival tactics ways, we learned how to endure a world stacked against us. Instead of asking *why* we needed protection, support, and understanding, the system chose to punish us.

The trauma we carry is not random. It's inherited. It's woven into the fabric of our communities through decades of neglect and deliberate harm. It's a legacy written in laws, policies, and practices designed to keep us confined. For many of us, this trauma became as natural as breathing. It shaped how we saw ourselves and how the world saw us. It created wounds that run deeper than any single moment of violence or loss—wounds that live in the silence of abandoned homes, in the fear behind locked doors, and in the quiet resignation that sometimes settles like dust in our hearts. This was segregation not just by geography but by design. A slow, deliberate stripping away of opportunity, hope, and humanity. And yet, even in this designed despair, we persisted. We loved, we dreamed, we fought. Because survival was never enough. We needed more than just to exist—we needed to be seen, heard, and valued.

A World Within Walls

Some places don't just raise you.

They mark you. Brand you. Shape the way you carry yourself in the world and the way the world receives you in return. Murphy Homes and Lexington Terrace—two names heavy with meaning in Baltimore's landscape. Not because they symbolized safety but because they became synonymous with abandonment. They weren't just housing projects. They were proof of what happens when people are boxed into corners and then left there—out of sight, out of policy, out of mind. Both projects were sinking under the same relentless pressure: violence, poverty, and neglect. But Lexington Terrace—my home—

was worse. By the time the city finally demolished it, only half the apartments were even livable. The rest stood like husks—boarded-up, caved-in, abandoned but not forgotten. Their silence was loud. Their windows were broken like missing teeth. You could hear echoes in those halls: sirens, arguments, prayers. Sometimes, nothing at all. Still, Lexington Terrace was more than just decaying brick and bad headlines. It was a world within walls. A place where, somehow, life still bloomed. Kids still played. Neighbors still looked out for one another. Joy made cameos in the most unexpected corners. We laughed in stairwells. We shared food between units. We made music out of chaos. Even as the buildings crumbled, we built community.

Afro American Newspapers/Gado. (1996, August 3). *Building at the Lexington Terrace housing project during demolition by implosion, Baltimore, Maryland. The original caption reads: "Lexington Terrace Public Housing, Al Cc 8/3/96 Blast #1"* [Photograph]. Getty Images.

https://www.gettyimages.com

The image of its demolition is seared into memory. A towering structure collapsing in on itself—a public declaration that the city had finally decided to erase what it once allowed to decay. But for those of us who lived there, the implosion didn't just tear down buildings. It took with it stories, struggles, pride, and pain—an entire era reduced to rubble and dust. And yet, the imprint remains. Not just in photos or memories but in how we move. How we see the world. Lexington Terrace wasn't just a place. It was the beginning. A wound. A badge.

A truth that still lives beneath the surface, no matter how many years or neighborhoods we travel away from it.

It was a pressure cooker. A world compressed by pain, fear, and relentless urgency. Childhood didn't stretch out in front of us with endless wonder. It ended early, sometimes before it even began. We learned to duck bullets before we learned how to ride bikes. We memorized the rhythm of gunfire before we ever mastered our ABCs. We read the tension in a neighbor's voice, the sharpness in footsteps, the way a door slammed the unspoken signs that danger was near. Playgrounds became battlegrounds. Swings rusted and cracked, clinging to chains that created stories of stolen innocence. And the parents, they grieved behind closed doors—quietly. They held their babies tight, not to smother, but because they knew that hope was fragile and often short-lived. Every single day was a whispered prayer:

Please let them come home. Please let them come home. Please let them come home.
Everything around us felt urgent Fast. Loud. Violent. The crackle of police radios. The hum of helicopters overhead. The sirens that never stopped. The shouting matches that could shift into murder with the wrong look or the wrong word. Even joy came with tension, like laughing on a landmine. A joke shared at the corner store could be interrupted by the sound of a gunshot. A basketball game under dim streetlights could turn into a memorial before the night was over. Those corner stores—with their flickering neon lights weren't just spots to buy candy or chips. They were at a crossroads. Places of survival, temptation, escape, and loss. Futures got shaped on those curbs. And then there were the vacant buildings. Hollowed-out bones of a city that had given up on us. They stood like ghosts, reminding us of what had been lost and warning us of what could never be reclaimed. Broken glass crunched beneath our sneakers. Walls peeled like scabs. Graffiti screamed stories no history book would ever print. But here's the part most people don't see:

Inside All That Pain, a World Still Lived

Inside all that pain, a world still lived—a world that refused to be extinguished, even beneath the weight of concrete and neglect. It was a world of resistance, built not from wealth but from will. Where laughter pierced silence like sunlight slipping through the cracks in boarded-up windows. Where music floated from second-story apartments, curling into the evening air like a prayer. Children chased joy down sidewalks as if they could outrun the shadows. And mothers—God, the mothers—held everything together with a strength that no one ever stopped to name, let alone honor. We didn't have much. But we had each other. We wove kinship from proximity, turned neighbors into family, survival into sacred rituals. When the city turned its back, we became each other's refuge. That kind of resilience was a quiet miracle. But miracles, too, have their costs. Survival is not the same as living. When you're always in survival mode, there's no room to simply *be*. You move through the world guarded. You hold your breath even when you're safe. You carry trauma in silence. You bury your dreams beneath the rubble of deferred hope. You learn to trust like a slow dance—tentative, measured. You love with caution and grieve behind closed doors, in the spaces where no one sees.

Lexington Terrace wasn't just a housing project—it was a crucible. It didn't merely house us; it forged us. Like fire, it shaped us as if we were steal. It gave us armor before we had language or words. Some of us made it out with our bodies intact. But few of us escaped with our hearts untouched. Because no matter how far you run, you carry the place that raised you. It's painful. It's pride. It's an unspoken lesson. You carry its walls even when you've left them behind. But here's the truth: those walls tried to contain our joy, our fury, our dreams. They failed. That spirit, born inside those walls, couldn't be caged. That spirit is what made me fight for something more. That's where transformation begins—not in the absence of struggle, but in the fire of it. In my first book, *I Found a Way Out*, I thanked God for my father. He was a constant presence in a world that often felt unstable. Every morning, he left for work early. Every afternoon, he came home at

4:30 p.m. sharp. That consistency was a lighthouse—a signal that not everything would fall apart. And my mother—she ran our home with military precision. Chores had to be done. Homework came first. Only then could we go outside and play. That order, that rhythm, gave me a sense of safety in the chaos. It taught me discipline. It taught me to care. And more than anything, it gave me perspective: that even in the struggle, there was love. There was structure. There was something worth holding on to. That clarity changed everything. I stopped seeing my circumstances as a prison. I started seeing them as preparation. Preparation for growth. For purpose. For the fight to rise again—even after I lost myself to the very environment I tried to outgrow. Because compassion isn't just kindness; it's surviving with your heart still open. Resilience isn't just endurance; it's choosing to hope when the world gives you every reason not to. And transformation, transformation doesn't happen in the absence of pain. It happens in the fire. In the ashes. In the choice to rise again, over and over. I made it through. Not unscathed. Not unchanged. But transformed. And I carry that spirit with me still.

Shaped by the Streets

Every single day felt like a trial. You didn't just walk through the neighborhood; you moved through a minefield. One wrong word, one wrong look, one step in the wrong direction could cost you everything. There was no manual. Just a brutal code passed down in whispers and warnings. Show no fear. Show no softness. Vulnerability wasn't an option—it was a target. You learned to wear a mask. To armor up. To keep your face unreadable and your heart guarded. Emotions were luxuries we couldn't afford. If you wanted to survive, you had to become something else—something colder, harder, sharper than what you were born to be. You couldn't just exist. You had to dominate. Or disappear.

For me, that meant chasing what looked like power. Not real power—the kind that brings peace or purpose—but the illusion of it. The kind that could momentarily shield you from pain or at least give you control over who could hurt you. Money. Cars. Reputation. The way people paused when you entered a room. The weight your name carried on certain blocks. I chased those things like they were lifelines. Like they could fill the empty spaces. If I could just wear the right designer labels, flash the right stack of bills, and grip the right wheel, maybe I'd finally matter. Maybe I'd finally be safe. But the safety I was chasing was a mirage. And the closer I got to it, the more it disappeared. What I didn't understand then was that no amount of surface-level power could protect you from what was already inside— the fear, the pain, the trauma you never had the space or language to process. Eventually, the streets reminded me of the price. I was shot. That bullet did more than tear into flesh. It carved something into my spirit—a cold, quiet reminder that the streets don't forgive. They don't forget. And they don't negotiate. They just take. They take your peace. Your people. Your sense of future. And if you're not careful, they take *you*.

Then came prison. Those cold walls, the buzz of fluorescent lights, the clang of metal doors—it was confinement, yes. But not just of my body. It was the logical next step of a life lived by rules I never chose but felt forced to follow. I wasn't just locked up by the state—I was imprisoned by a belief system I had inherited and internalized: that this was all I was worth. That this was all I could ever expect. I lost friends. Not just to bullets but to slower deaths. Quiet ones. Bitterness that hardened their hearts until they couldn't feel anything at all. Drugs that blurred the edges of unbearable realities. Depression that moved in like fog and never left. We didn't talk about mental health. We didn't have therapists or language for trauma. We just kept going—numb, angry, exhausted. Pretending silence was strength. Pretending survival was the same as healing. It wasn't. The cost of becoming who I thought I had to be wasn't just physical. It was emotional. Spiritual. The erosion of trust. The numbing of empathy. The slow surrender of parts of myself I hadn't even named yet. And for a long time, I didn't question it—because the streets were all I knew. They were my map. My mentor. My mythology. My trap. But there's something that happens in the quiet after the chaos, in the silence that follows the sirens. When the dust settles, and you're left alone with your thoughts—those unspoken parts of you that never stopped aching—you start to realize that surviving the streets isn't the same as escaping them. And it's definitely not the same as living. I began to understand that freedom wasn't just about walking away. It was about unlearning. About breaking the code. About refusing to keep living by rules that were never meant to keep us whole. It meant reclaiming myself—my softness, my vulnerability, my right to feel, to dream, to hope. The streets shaped me. No doubt about that. But they didn't finish me.

When Death Becomes Normal

I watched people die like it was just another part of life. Bodies— broken, still, fading into the same cracked pavement where we once ran barefoot, chasing ice cream trucks and distant dreams. Sidewalks that should've held the laughter of childhood instead held blood. The corners where we learned how to play were the same places we learned how to grieve. Innocence never had a chance.

Yellow police tape stretched across the neighborhood like caution-colored curtains, pulled back and forth so often they stopped meaning anything. It became background scenery—like traffic lights, corner stores, and chain-link fences. You stopped noticing it because it was always there. Gunshots didn't scare us anymore. They weren't shocking. They weren't even surprising. They were ambient noise. Like sirens, like barking dogs, like mothers yelling out windows for their kids to come inside. When the shots rang out, we didn't scream. We paused. We ducked. Then we kept moving. As if violence was just part of the rhythm of our lives, like some cruel choreography we all knew by heart. But the real horror wasn't the blood. It wasn't the funerals or the sirens. It was *normalcy*. How quickly death stopped feeling like an interruption and started feeling like a fact. Something expected. Anticipated. Inescapable. That's what haunted me. The silence that followed gunfire was never empty. It was full—thick with the weight of everything we didn't say. We didn't cry anymore. Tears were for people with time, with space, with the privilege to feel without breaking. We didn't ask questions either because there were never any answers. And when there were, they didn't change anything. The dead stayed dead.

Hope was something we learned to hide. It felt dangerous to believe things could be different. Because hope meant wanting. Wanting meant caring. And caring made you vulnerable. So, we buried it—deep. Tucked it away like an old toy you were too afraid to lose again. Grief became a private ritual. You did it alone. Behind closed doors. In the quiet spaces between the school and the street. We wore our pain like armor, tough on the outside, trembling underneath. We learned to steady our faces while our hearts fractured. To smile without softness. To carry loss in silence. But it wasn't just the lives we lost. It was the future. Childhoods. Versions of ourselves that never had a chance to become. Each death carved another piece out of us. Not all at once—but slowly. Like erosion. A crack here, a shift there. Until one day, you woke up and realized you no longer remembered who you were before the grief. Still, life went on. Not because we were okay—but because we had to. The Lexington Terrence didn't just shape how we lived—it shaped how we *survived*. And in that survival, we learned to carry death like a shadow. Always just behind us. Never gone. Always close. For a long time, I thought it was just me—jumping at loud sounds, always watching exits, never fully relaxing, even in so-called safe spaces. I thought I was just wired wrong. But I wasn't.

A 2016 study on young Black men in Baltimore who had lost someone to homicide found that more than 70% reported symptoms of PTSD. Seventy percent. But nobody in our neighborhoods called it that. We didn't say "trauma." We said things like, "I stay on point." That was our diagnosis. Hypervigilance. Emotional shutdown. Nightmares. Rage. But it didn't show up on a clipboard. It showed up in our personalities. In our relationships. In the way, we raised our voices or didn't raise them at all. In a world where there is no "post" in post-traumatic stress, the trauma never ends. It just becomes part of you. We never had the luxury of healing. We only had the instinct to keep going. To walk through life carrying both grief and grit in equal measure. And somehow, we did. But even now, even years later, I still feel it. In the way, I scan a room. In the way, I sleep with one eye open. In the way, I carry the names of the dead like prayer beads in my mind. Death became normal. But we were never meant to get used to it. And I think part of healing means finally saying that out loud.

Chapter Two
The Script I Didn't Write

I lived by a script I never wrote.

It was handed to me before I ever took my first breath—quietly, almost invisibly, passed down through generations. Shaped by the weight of history. Stitched together by policy, poverty, and prejudice. It came not as a conversation but as an inheritance. An unspoken contract written in red lines on city maps, in underfunded schools, in over-policed streets and in under-resourced homes. Before I could crawl, the world had already decided who I was supposed to be. And like so many kids born in places like Lexington Terrace, I stepped into the role without question. We all did. The streets had their own script for us: *Be hard. Be feared. Don't feel. Don't dream.* Every move felt predestined. Every choice is confined to narrow streets and hallways with no exits. It wasn't just the environment—it was the expectation.

A story being lived out around us every day. Our lines were written in violence and silence. Inside glances and survival. You learn quickly that the streets don't offer many endings. You die young. You disappear behind bars. Or you find a way to forget that either fate could be yours at any moment. Those weren't just fears. They were forecasts. I followed the script for a long time because I didn't know there was another one. I chased the illusion of power—money, reputation, fear-based respect. I wore toughness-like armor and mistook numbness for strength. I believed the lies because no one had ever told me anything else. Because when a lie is repeated enough times, in enough lives, it begins to feel like truth. Then, one day, I had an epiphany.

Maybe it was a whisper in the chaos. Maybe it was the mirror refusing to lie back. Maybe it was the weight of too many funerals, too many nights behind locked doors, too many moments when I couldn't recognize myself anymore. But there it was: the realization that this script only ends in one of two ways—a grave or a cage. And I had already tasted both. I'd felt the fire of bullets tear through my flesh, seeing blood spill where children once played. I'd stood in handcuffs while the world looked away. Heard the heavy thud of prison doors locking behind me. Tasted the bitterness of being reduced to a number. I knew what it meant to vanish from your own life, to be alive but no longer free. That's when the question rose up in me like a flood I couldn't stop:

Is this all I am? Is this all I get?

The answer didn't come easy. It didn't come loud or clear. It came quietly, wrapped in shame and sorrow. It came in tears I thought I no longer had; in memories, I tried to outrun. But it came. And with it, a flicker of something else. Hunger. A refusal to die living out a role I never chose. By some grace—some divine intervention, or maybe just a raw, stubborn will—I began to break away. Not just from the streets but from the narrative itself. Because the real escape wasn't physical; it was spiritual. Emotional. It was an act of rebellion against the destiny I'd been handed. It was a declaration:

I am not what happened to me. I am not the role I was forced to play. I am the author of what comes next. Every day since has been part of that rewrite. Some days, the old script still whispers. Some days, I still carry its rhythm in my walk, its survival code in my instincts. The weight of the past doesn't disappear just because you decide to rise. But here's the difference: now, I carry a pen in my hand. Not just scars on my body. And with that pen, I am writing a different story—not just for myself, but for anyone who was ever told they had no choice. Anyone who was ever handed a role they never auditioned for.

I didn't choose the script I was given. But I choose *now*. To be the author of a life worth living. Life is not defined by how it began but by how it transforms.

Healing Is Not What They Told Us

People talk about healing like it's soft. Like it's candles and lavender. Like its gentle yoga poses and warm tea. Like it's sitting quietly in the sun, letting your pain melt away while peace washes over you in waves. But that's not how healing came for me. It didn't whisper. It *roared*. It didn't cradle me—it cracked me open. Healing, for me, was violent. Not the kind of violence I grew up with, not fists slamming against skin or bullets echoing through alleyways. Not the kind you could see in police reports or count in obituaries. This violence lived inside. Quiet for a long time, then suddenly. Brutal. A force that pulled me back into every fire I thought I had already escaped. Healing doesn't knock. It kicks the door off the hinges. It comes for everything you tried to bury: the grief you never cried for, the guilt you never named, the rage you never admitted, and the silence you wore like armor. It drags up the memories you tried to drink away, smoke away, fight away. It lays them all out in front of you dares you to look. Not to punish you—but to *free* you. Because here's the truth no one told me:

You can't heal what you refuse to face.

Real healing is looking at yourself in the mirror—eyes swollen, hands shaking, heart splintered—and saying, "I see you. And I'm staying." It's not peaceful. It's not graceful. It's not clean. It's a war. A war for your soul. A battle for your future. And most of that battle is fought in silence. Behind closed doors. In the small hours of the morning when the weight of your past presses on your chest like a hand that won't let you breathe. When your body remembers things, your mind tries to forget. When the tears come, and you don't know why, your only choice is to let them fall. Healing is not an Instagram post. It's not a hashtag. It breaks down in the same places where you used to feel proud. It's sitting in a room alone, trying not to run from yourself. It's learning to let your body feel—really *feel*—the ache you've numbed for years. It's the shame that rises, the flashbacks that shake you, the old voices that echo louder when everything else gets quiet. And yet—even in that chaos—there's something sacred happening. Because of that violence, that storm, *it's not the end*. It's the beginning. Real healing doesn't just patch you up. It doesn't put a bandage over bullet holes. It *rebuilds* you.

But first, it has to tear. First, it has to strip you down to what's real. It has to unmake the lies you told yourself just to survive. It has to clear the wreckage of who the world said you had to be. Only then can something honest begin to grow. On the other side of that breaking, there's breath. There's clarity. There's life. Not the life someone scripted for you. Not the one you chased to feel safe. But the one that's yours. The one where you're no longer surviving your pain—you're *transforming* through it. And that kind of healing. That kind of freedom. It's worth every tear. Every fight. Every night, you thought you wouldn't make it.

Because once you walk through that fire and come out on the other side, you don't just *live*—you rise.

Confronting the Ghosts

Healing meant I had to sit with the ghosts I spent my whole life outrunning. Not just the ghosts of people I lost—but the ones I *became*. The versions of me I had to construct just to survive. The ones who knew how to laugh through pain, how to turn fear into fury, how to wear hardness like a second skin. I became a master of disguise. Quick with a joke, sharp with a stare. I learned to mask my tenderness behind toughness because I thought it was the only way to stay alive. I thought leaving the streets would be enough. Once I got out, the ghosts would stay behind. But some of them followed. Not in the body—but in memory. In habits. In the quiet reflexes that never really left. They haunted the corners of my mind and whispered in moments of stillness. They showed up in the way I flinched when someone got too close with kindness. In the way, I prepared for the worst, even when everything around me said I was finally safe. They lived in my distrust, in my detachment, in the way I kept people at arm's length—not because I didn't want love, but because I never learned how to trust it.

There were faces I couldn't forget. Friends I buried too young. Names I stopped saying out loud because they hurt too much to hold in my mouth. Boys who should've been in classrooms or on playgrounds—but instead ended up in caskets or cages. We shared childhoods stolen by bullets, broken by systems, and silenced by a world that never expected us to grow old. Their absence clung to me like a second skin. Even in moments of healing, they were still with me. Confronting those ghosts meant reliving what I spent years trying to bury. Gunshots that shattered the night. Sirens that became lullabies. The screams that lingered long after the violence ended. The sound of a mother collapsing to her knees when her child didn't come home. These weren't stories I read—they were memories I carried in my bones. And then there was the night I thought would be my last. And the ones that followed, when I didn't care if it was. But maybe the hardest ghost to face wasn't someone I lost. It was someone I used to be. The boy who had dreams before the world crushed them. The boy who still believed in people. Who smiled without suspicion. Who loved without fear. The boy never really got to *be* a child because he was too busy learning how not to die. I cried for him. I raged for him. I *grieved* him.

Because no one ever tells you how heavy it is to mourn the version of yourself you had to kill just to make it through. No one prepares you for the ache that comes from knowing you had to let go of your softness to survive. Healing made me confront what survival *costs*. And some days, that pain was heavier than any bullet. Heavier than any sentence.
Heavier than any fight I ever had in the streets. But when I stopped running—when I sat still with those ghosts, face to face, heart to heart—something changed. Not peace. Not right away. But truth. And with that truth came something I never thought I'd find: compassion.

Not just for the ones I lost—but for myself. Because healing isn't always about moving on, sometimes, it's about *returning*—to the parts of yourself you thought were gone. Sometimes, it means sitting with the shattered pieces and saying: "I see you. You did what you had to do. And now… you can rest." That's where healing really began for me—not in forgetting, but in *forgiving*. Not in pretending the past didn't happen but in allowing the pain to breathe. And in that breath, I found something like freedom.

Tearing Down the Walls

In the streets, I learned early walls keep you alive. Not just the concrete ones that surrounded our buildings—but the invisible ones we built around ourselves. Walls around the heart. Walls around emotion. Walls around the truth. Out there, the vulnerability was dangerous. Softness could get you jumped. Tears were like blood in the water. So you learned to lock it all down. You learned to hide what hurt. You laugh when you want to cry.

You fight when you really want to run. You say, *"I'm good,"* even when you're dying inside. You numb yourself just enough to function—because in that world, survival wasn't about feeling. It was about *displaying strength*, no matter the cost. That's what the streets taught me: how to wear masks so well I forgot who I was underneath. I wore my armor-like skin—cold, thick, impenetrable. I kept my guard up with everyone, even the ones who meant well. Trust was a risk I couldn't afford. Love was a luxury I couldn't understand. So, I stayed closed off. Silent. Sharp. Safe. But healing doesn't happen behind walls. Healing doesn't reward performance; it demands presence. It asks for your truth, not your toughness. And that's something the streets never prepared me for. Healing demanded that

I feel. It required me to open the door and let the pain in. Not so it could destroy me—but so it could *clean* the wounds I had ignored for years. Pain, unaddressed, doesn't disappear. It calcifies. It turns into anger, into avoidance, into habits that feel like personality but are really just survival tactics.

Taking down those walls wasn't poetic. It wasn't graceful. It was terrifying. Because those walls *protected* me, they were the only reason I made it through. Without them, I felt exposed. Raw. Like standing naked in a storm. But brick by brick, I started to dismantle the fortress I'd built around my heart. Not all at once. Not without resistance. But slowly—through tears, I had held back for decades. Through truths, I finally said out loud. Through memories, I stopped running. And with every wall that came down, I found something I didn't expect: **Myself.**

Not the version the streets demanded. Not the one hardened by fear or shaped by survival. But the one I buried a long time ago, the one who still wanted to love, to be loved. The one who didn't need to exhibit toughness to prove he was worthy. Healing didn't ask me to forget where I came from. It didn't ask me to erase the past. It asked me to *become more* than what hurt me. To stop protecting my pain like it was a treasure and start honoring my truth like it was sacred. And that truth, it was messy. It was inconvenient. It was vulnerable. But it was mine. To heal, I had to be honest. And honesty, for someone like me, felt like bleeding in public. But only when I let myself bleed did I finally begin to breathe.

The Loneliness of Becoming New

Transformation costs. And one of the first things it costs is connection. There's a silence that comes with healing. Not the peaceful kind—the kind people write poems about. No. This silence echoes. It empties rooms. It turns familiar laughter into distant memories. Because when you start to change—really change—not everyone comes with you. When you choose peace over chaos, Growth over survival, Truth over comfort—Some people don't recognize you anymore. And it's not always malice. Sometimes, they just don't know how to love the version of you that isn't bleeding any more. The hardest part isn't always losing them. It's realizing they may have only loved the broken version of you. The version that was always available to carry their weight. Always in pain but never complaining. Always playing a role that made *them* feel safe, even when it cost me everything. But healing stripped that mask away. It didn't just change how I lived—it changed who I was. And for a while, even I didn't recognize the person staring back at me. There were nights when healing felt lonelier than prison. Because at least in prison, I knew the rules. I knew my place. I knew which version of me needed to show up to survive. But out here—in this new life I was trying to build— there was no script. No armor. No applause for becoming someone softer, more whole. Just me. Raw. Unsure. Vulnerable. Trying to learn how to live, not just exist. There's a strange kind of grief in becoming new. You mourn the people you had to leave behind. You miss the chaos you once mistook for connection. You even miss the old you— The one who knew how to navigate pain like it was home, even when that version of you was exhausted. Even when that version was dying slowly. But I kept going. Even when no one understood me. Even when the silence screamed louder than any siren ever had. Because I knew what going back would cost. Going back would mean betrayal— Not just of the man I was becoming, but of the little boy inside me who used to dream of *more*. Going back meant pretending again. It meant shrinking. It meant erasing everything I fought to reclaim. And I didn't come this far just to disappear into someone else's comfort zone. So, I learned to sit in the quiet. Feel the ache of isolation without rushing to escape it. To treat loneliness not as failure, but as proof that I was no longer living a lie. I began to trust that letting go—truly letting go—would eventually lead me to something real. Something true. Something I deserved. Because sometimes, becoming who you *really are* requires walking away from everything you *used to be*. Even if it means walking alone—for a while.

Worthy of Wholeness

The hardest kind of love—the kind that nearly broke me trying to learn— was the love I owed to myself. For so long, I believed I didn't deserve peace. Not after the things I'd done. Not after the blood I'd seen spilled or the choices I made while trying to survive. I carried shame like a second skin. I wore guilt-like armor. Some part of me believed the world was right— That I was too broken, too far gone, too soaked in mistakes to ever be whole again. I thought wholeness was for other people. People who hadn't lived in survival mode. People who hadn't been caged by poverty, violence, or prison walls.

People who hadn't buried friends before they turned twenty. The weight of my past felt permanent—like a sentence written in a language I wasn't allowed to rewrite. I had internalized the lies the world fed me: That I was less than. That I was my worst day that I was damaged in human form. Disposable. Forgettable. Beyond redemption. But healing—slow, unglamorous, and relentless—taught me a different truth. It didn't come loud. It came in whispers. Soft, steady, insistent: You are not your worst mistake. You are not the sum of your scars. You are not the violence that tried to shape you. You are not the trauma the system assumed you'd never outlive. You are more. You are *still here*. And that is not small. That is sacred.

Healing didn't erase the pain—it reframed it. It showed me that survival was not shameful but evidence of resilience. That the cracks in me weren't proof I was ruined but proof that I held together under pressure that should have shattered me. It showed me that being whole didn't mean being untouched by pain. It meant refusing to be defined by it.

Wholeness, I learned, isn't a reward for perfection. It's a birthright. It's the quiet truth that lives underneath the rubble of trauma: That you were always worthy of love, even when no one told you. Even when you couldn't say it to yourself. Healing is reclaiming that truth. It's seeing your reflection and no longer only counting the wounds. It's being able to say:

"I deserve peace. I deserve love. I deserve to feel joy—without apology, without condition."

That realization—simple and radical— can start a revolution inside your soul. Because in a world that profits off your brokenness, choosing to love yourself—to see yourself as worthy of healing, worthy of softness, worthy of a future—is not just personal. It's political. It's spiritual. It's liberation. You deserve to be whole. Not someday. Not if the world finally decides you've done enough to earn it. Right now. As you are. And that truth, when you let it in— that unshakable, undeniable truth— is where real healing begins.

The Fight That Never Ends

Healing is not a destination. It's not some mountaintop you reach where the pain suddenly disappears. It's not a neat, linear journey. It's a war—a quiet one. Fought in the privacy of your mind, your body, your spirit. Healing doesn't come wrapped in closure or clarity. It doesn't promise you peace forever. It demands your presence—*daily*. Because even after you've changed your life, even after you've broken the cycles, even after you've walked away from the street, the trauma doesn't disappear. It lingers. In your reflexes. In your dreams. In your silence. Some mornings, I wake up and feel it rising like a tide—the old voices trying to find their way back in: "You're still that kid from the block." "You'll never outrun what you've done." "You don't belong in this new life." They're whispers now—but some days, they still shout. That's the thing no one tells you: The fight never really ends. You just get stronger. Wiser. More equipped. I used to think healing meant never feeling broken again. Now I know—it means being willing to keep going *even when you feel broken*. It means choosing the truth when the lies come crawling back. It means remembering who you are, not who the world tried to make you. Yes, the pain still visits. Yes, I still carry grief.

Yes, there are days I question my worth, my progress, my path.

But I also carry something I didn't have before: Tools. Truths I fought for. Breath worth. Boundaries. Prayer. Writing. Self-forgiveness that I had to learn the hard way. Love I now know how to receive. I carry strength—not the kind I used to perform to stay alive, but the kind born from sitting with my wounds instead of hiding them. The kind that says, *"I can feel this and still be free."* The streets taught me how to survive. How to armor up. How to move through danger. How to never flinch. But healing, healing is teaching me how to live. Fully. Present. Honest. Without the mask. And that is the real fight. Not just staying alive but learning to believe I *deserve* to be. So, no, the fight doesn't end. But neither does the rising. And every time I choose truth over fear, softness over shame, presence over numbness, I win. Not just for me. But for the boy, I used to be. For the ones who didn't make it. For the future, I refuse to abandon. This is what the fight looks like now. It's quieter. But it's deeper. And this time—*I know I'm winning.*

Reclaiming My Life, Rewriting My Ending

This isn't just a story of escape. It's a story of reclamation. Of going back—not to stay trapped in the past, but to gather the pieces of myself I once abandoned. The pieces I thought were gone forever. The parts I had to bury just to make it through. For years, I believed survival was the goal. That making it out alive was enough. But surviving isn't the same as living. And freedom isn't just the absence of chains. It's the presence of choice.

Of peace. Of *purpose*. This journey has been more than just leaving something behind—it's been about returning to myself. To the soft, brave, brilliant boy I had to hide. To the dreams, I stuffed down under concrete and chaos. To tell the truth, I was taught by my parents to speak out loud. I used to think my pain was a period—the end of the sentence. But I see now it was a comma. A pause. A breath. The beginning of my purpose. The violence, the loss, the grief that once felt like proof that I was cursed—I've turned them into fuel. Fuel for healing. Fuel for creating. Fuel for helping others find the light in their own darkness. Yes, I survived. But survival was just the first chapter. The real transformation came when I chose not just to get out—but to go through. Through the shadows. Through the rage. Through the memories that haunted me. Through the silence, I wrapped around my wounds. Through the stories, I was handed to the one I finally had the courage to write for myself.

That's what *I Found a Way Out* really means. It's not just about escaping the streets. It's about never letting the streets define me again. It's about resurrection—not just of the body, but of the spirit. It's about refusing to be limited by what happened to me and instead using it as a foundation for what I'm building now. This is a story of hope shaped by hardship, of strength that didn't come easy, and of a life reclaimed—not handed, not borrowed, but *owned*. This is a story for anyone who feels like they're too far gone. Too broken. Too late. It's proof that the past doesn't get to dictate your future. That no matter how far you've fallen, no matter how deep the hole, *you can still rise.* Because sometimes, the most powerful thing you'll ever do is *pick up the pen*, look your pain in the face, and say:

"This is not how my story ends."

Chapter Three
Haunted by Yesterday's Fighting
for Tomorrow

If you met me today — passed me on the street, crossed paths in a quiet café, or shared a few words in line at the grocery store — you might walk away thinking, "He seems so peaceful." You might say I look grounded, maybe even wise. You'd notice how I sit in silence, how I don't fill empty spaces with noise just to prove I'm here. You might pick up on the quiet calm that follows me, not flashy or loud, but steady, like something earned after years of chaos. You'd be right to notice that stillness. But you'd only be seeing the surface. Because of this calm, you see in me now — this gentleness, this grace — it wasn't handed down like an heirloom. It wasn't some natural part of me that was always there. No. What you see now was built. Brick by brick. Scar by scar. It was fought for. Prayed over. Wept into the floorboards of nights that had no end. This peace came with a cost. One that only I truly know. There were days when I couldn't find silence without finding pain. Nights when the quiet didn't comfort me — it cornered me. It echoed with every name I was called, every fight I barely survived, every part of myself I had to lock away just to make it to morning. I know what it's like to sit in a room so still it feels like the walls are leaning in, listening, daring you to fall apart. I've lived through moments where my own thoughts were louder than any chaos around me, and the worst part was knowing I had no idea how to silence them.

The truth is, I didn't always want peace. I didn't even know what it looked like. For a long time, all I knew was survival. I was forged in fire, shaped by trauma, and taught that strength looked like never flinching. Never crying. Never break. I was loud because I was scared. I was angry because I was hurting. I wore pride-like armor because I was so tired of being seen as weak — tired of being seen at all. And yet, underneath all that noise, I was just a boy aching for rest. I was exhausted. But I didn't know how to say, "I'm tired." Because where I came from, tired looked like weakness. And weakness, that could get you hurt. Or worse. The man you see now, he was born the moment I stopped pretending I was fine. The moment I sat on the edge of a bed that had held more pain than peace and asked myself — not out loud, but loud enough to shake something in me — "Is this it?" "Is this all I'm ever going to be?" That was the crack in the armor. Not a dramatic moment. No sirens, no rock bottom. Just a quiet breaking. A sacred unraveling. And that's where change began — not in an explosion, but in a whisper. From that moment on, I started walking away. Not from my past but from the need to be defined by it. I began letting go of who I had to be just to survive and reaching — slowly, painfully — toward who I could become. I laid down the noise. I picked up quiet. I learned to breathe. I started healing. I started telling the truth — even the hard parts. Especially the hard parts. Stillness felt dangerous at first. When you've lived your life in storms, peace can feel like a trap. But I stayed. I stayed, and I listened. And in the quiet, a voice rose up from somewhere deep inside, somewhere I had long forgotten. "You were made for more."

So, if you see me now and think I'm calm, you're seeing a man who's made peace with his own war. If you see gentleness, you're seeing someone who finally understands that strength has nothing to do with how loud you are — and everything to do with how deeply you love. If you feel stillness from me, know it's because I no longer run from myself. And if you think I'm peaceful, then maybe you're finally seeing not just the man I became… But the boy who fought like hell to become him.

The Weight of Silence

There were times when silence didn't soothe me — it swallowed me. Not every quiet is sacred. Some quiets ache. I've sat in rooms where the lights were off, but everything inside me was lit up in chaos. Rooms where the silence didn't offer peace, only pressure. Where the walls felt like they were leaning in, and the ceiling hovered just low enough to make breathing feel like a sin. There were no voices, no sounds — just the weight of everything I'd been avoiding crashing down at once. And in that kind of silence, sleep isn't mercy. It's a memory. I'd lay in beds that felt like battlegrounds, sheets tangled like chains. Nights didn't bring rest — they brought reckoning. Regret would show up like a ghost with my face, my voice, my past. And it would whisper things I thought I had buried. Every wrong choice. Every unspoken apology. Every version of me I had to become just to survive.

That kind of silence isn't quiet at all. It screams — louder than fists, sharper than words, more brutal than any fight I ever swung my way through. You wouldn't have recognized me then. I wasn't soft. I wasn't still. I was hard and loud and coiled so tight that even kindness could feel like a threat. I was someone who walked like a weapon and talked like a warning. I wasn't just a fighter in body — I was a fighter in spirit, in soul. Not because I wanted to be… but because I didn't think I had a choice. I was forged in fire. Shaped by pain. Tempered by trauma and street logic. In the world I came from, survival wasn't promised — it was earned. And to earn it, you had to build yourself into something no one could touch. Tired. That was a weakness. Sad. That got you laughed at or left behind. Vulnerable. That could get you killed. So, I didn't show it. Not the fatigue. Not the fear. Not the desperate ache I carried like a second skin. I buried it. Swallowed it. Camouflaged it with bravado and rage and a voice that never broke, even when my spirit did. Because where I was from, the world didn't make space for soft men. But that silence — the kind that haunted, not healed —broke something open in me. Slowly. Quietly. The very thing I feared about silence became the thing that saved me. It made me listen. To the echoes inside. To the child, I'd silenced. To the grief, I hadn't grieved.

And somewhere in all that unbearable quiet, I started to feel the faintest pulse of something unfamiliar — not weakness. Not defeat. Hope.

The road from that man to the one standing here now wasn't straight. It wasn't clean. And it sure as hell wasn't easy. But that silence, the kind that once threatened to undo me, became the ground I rebuilt myself on. So, when you see me today — calm, still, composed — know that you're not just seeing a man who knows peace. You're seeing a man who wrestled with the weight of silence… And lived long enough to find its grace.

The Breaking Point

Change doesn't always come wrapped in drama. It doesn't always crash in with sirens or explosions or a moment so loud you remember it like a movie scene. No. Sometimes, change enters soft and unnoticed — like a breath you didn't realize you were holding. Like a sigh that finally breaks the silence. I remember the moment my life started to shift.

It wasn't bloody. It wasn't loud. It wasn't even particularly dramatic from the outside looking in. But it was the most honest moment I had ever had with myself. There were no gunshots echoing down the block that night. No screaming. No chasing headlights. Just me. Alone. Sitting on the edge of a bed that had forgotten what rest felt like. A bed that had held my body but never comforted my soul. I hadn't truly slept in what felt like forever — only passed out, only shut down. Nights were never for dreaming. They were for dodging demons. And in that stillness, with my heart beating like a fist against my chest and my mind running like it was on fire, something broke open. Four walls. One body. A thousand regrets. And one single thought — so clear, it split me open: *"Is this all I'm ever going to be?"* It echoed through me like thunder. Not loud in the room, but deafening in my spirit. *"Is this it?"*

41

That question didn't fix me. It didn't magically make the trauma dissolve or erase the years I'd lived in armor. But it *cracked* something. Cracked it wide enough for a flicker of something I hadn't felt in a long, long time — maybe ever. Hope. Not the big movie kind. Not the kind with sweeping music and happy endings.

But the quiet kind. The kind that shows up in whispers, not roars. The kind that says, *maybe*. Maybe you don't have to stay like this. Maybe the fire burning you from the inside out isn't the only warmth you'll ever know. Maybe what's next doesn't have to look like what came before. That night, nothing outside changed. No phone call came to save me. No one knocked on the door with answers. I was still in that same room, still in that same skin. But inside, something shifted. Something said, *Get up*. And so, I did. That was the beginning. The beginning of the long walk home to myself. The walk away from the corners and chaos I'd once called safety. The walk away from the masks I'd worn so long they'd nearly become my skin. The walk away from pain — not because I wasn't still carrying it, but because I had finally decided to carry it differently. That moment was small. But it was sacred. Because that's when I finally stopped surviving long enough to imagine something more. And that's all it takes sometimes — just one honest breath. One true question. One fragile, trembling crack in the wall you swore you'd never let fall. Enough for the light to get in. Enough for truth to whisper louder than fear. Enough to begin. That's when I started walking. Not fast. Not far. But forward. And for the first time… I wasn't running.

Away from the Fire

I didn't walk away at all at once. There was no grand exit, no cinematic break from the past. It was slower than that. More like unraveling — one frayed thread at a time. I started letting go. Not in a blaze of glory but in the quiet, almost invisible moments. The moments when I stopped answering the call to prove myself. The moments when I stopped fueling the fire inside me with anger, with pride, with the relentless need to be seen as unbreakable. I began to release the weight I'd been carrying — the weight of expectations, the weight of pain, the weight of survival. I stepped away from the noise — that constant, pounding soundtrack of posturing and toughness and fights that never ended. I let go of the mask I wore so tightly, the one that said, "I'm ready. I'm strong. I'm unshakable." I laid down my armor, piece by piece, even though every fiber of my being screamed at me that doing so was dangerous. Because letting go meant becoming vulnerable — and vulnerability felt like standing in the middle of a battlefield with no shield. Instead of noise, I picked up silence. But not the kind of silence that haunted me — the silence that pressed on my chest, trapping my breath, dragging me deeper into shadows. No. This was a different silence. A silence that didn't threaten me. A silence that held space. A silence that wrapped around me like a soft blanket instead of a cold chain. A silence that invited healing instead of stirring up old wounds. The stillness was terrifying. Because when you've lived inside storms your whole life, peace feels like danger. It feels like bait. Like a trap waiting to snap shut.

You want to run back to the chaos, to the noise, to the familiar pain — even if it's brutal — because at least it's known. But that night, that moment, I stayed. I stayed still enough to hear a voice — soft, quiet, almost buried beneath the clamor of survival — a voice I hadn't heard in years. A voice that spoke gently, insistently: *"You were made for more."* Those words weren't just hope. They were a call. A promise. A truth. I wasn't broken beyond repair. I wasn't destined to live in shadow forever. I was more than the fire I'd escaped. More than the man I'd been forced to become. More than the pain I had endured. I was someone who could breathe again. Someone who could choose differently. Someone who could be whole. And so I stayed I stayed with that quietness, that stillness, until it became strength. Until it became peace. I walked away from the fire. Not because it was not a part of me — it always would be. But because I was done letting it burn me alive. I was ready to build something new from the ashes.

What Healing Looks Like

Now, I am still in the process. Still becoming. Still learning — sometimes with grace, sometimes with grit. Sometimes, with hands trembling but still reaching anyway. Healing, I have found, is not a clean arc. It does not arrive like sunlight through a window. It creeps in — soft, slow, persistent — like green pushing through concrete. Like breath returning after years of holding it. I am still shedding old skin, like a tree that loses its leaves not once, But over and over — Letting go so new growth has a place to land.

Healing is circular like that —A loop, not a ladder. One day steady, the next unraveling. But each time, I come back to myself more whole than before. Each morning now, I make a quiet choice: Peace over pride. Healing over habit. Softness over the armor I once wore like a second skin. Because where I come from, hardness kept you safe. But it also kept you numb. I'm learning now to be gentle with myself —To hold my own wounds with tenderness Instead of shame. To speak to my own reflection with the kind of love I once believed I had to earn. Because gentleness isn't weakness, it's power — Fierce, rooted, and unshakable. The kind of power that doesn't need to shout to be heard. That doesn't swing fists but still stands firm. The kind that allows tears *without* apology. That says: "I don't have to be invincible to be worthy." I'm learning that real silence — The kind that isn't empty but full — is sacred.

A silence that holds space for grief. For breath. For memory. For peace. It's not the silence of trauma that screams in the absence of safety. Not the silence I used to wear like camouflage to survive loud streets and louder systems. This is different. This is the silence of presence.

The silence of finally feeling *safe enough* to be still. And maybe the most important thing I'm learning is that I am enough. Not because of what I've accomplished. Not because of what I've endured. Not because I turned pain into poetry. But simply because I *am*. Breathing. Trying. Growing. Existing with intention. And that is sacred, too. Even now — Even in the soft, quiet moments — Peace can still be disrupted. A name said too sharply. A glance that feels like a memory. A shadow that slips through the cracks in the door of the present. And in those moments, the ground beneath me feels shaky again. I remember I'm still human. Still fragile. Still healing. But now, now, I have tools. Not the tools they handed me in the streets — The silence, the fists, the side-eyes, the exits. I carry new tools now. The breath. The boundary. The ability to pause instead of reacting. To remember who I am beneath the noise, Beneath the name-calling, beneath the old scripts. And I choose peace again. Even when it feels hard. Even when I have to start over. Again and again and again. Because healing doesn't mean I never fall, it means I rise differently. With intention.

With softness. With power.

Chapter Four
When the Past Calls My Name

It always comes suddenly. A voice from behind, casual but sharp — "Yo, Jim!" And just like that, the air thickens. The calm I've built — carefully, day by day — trembles. My breath shortens; my chest tightens. Something shifts inside me, old and automatic. My shoulders rise before I even know why. The old armor slides on like it never left. Because that name — Jim Hart —isn't just a name. It's a trigger. A summons. A spark that lights a fuse I've spent years trying to snuff out. It's a sound that carries weight — Not just syllables, but history. Concrete and sirens. Fists and fear. Silence and survival. When my family says it, it lands soft. It's threaded with memory, layered with love. It's their way of saying:

"We see you — not just who you are now, but who you were. We remember the boy who made it out." That version of "Jim" feels like home. Safe. Sacred. But when it comes from someone else —From the streets, From the shadows I left behind, From the ones still locked in the old code —It means something else entirely. It's not a name. It's a test. A challenge. They're not asking how I am. They're asking if I'm still built the same. If the heat still lives under my skin. If the old rage still breathes beneath this steady surface. They're looking for a flicker. A crack. Waiting to see if I'll snap back, if I'll step back into that old skin like I never outgrew it. But I have. I had to.

Because *that Jim* —The one who could fight before he could speak his feelings —Was necessary in a world that didn't offer safety. He was armor in a battlefield of cracked sidewalks, locked gates, and eyes that never looked at you — only through you. He kept me alive. But he wasn't built for peace. He wasn't built for rest. He wasn't built to grow. I left that version of me behind — not in shame, But in truth. I left because I finally saw that survival is not the same as living. And leaving wasn't easy. It was painful. Deliberate. Like peeling away skin to find something softer underneath. There were nights I sat alone in silence so thick it echoed. Nights where the urge to go back were louder than the reasons I left. But I stayed. I breathed through it. I chose healing, even when it felt like a loss. So when that voice calls out — "Jim!" — I don't just hear the sound. I hear weight. I hear the streets I've buried. I hear violence in the shape of memory. I hear the ghosts trying to pull me back through the doors I locked in a reason. And in that moment, I paused. Feel the tightness rise. Feel the pull. And I say, not out loud but loud enough for my soul to hear:

"Boy, don't you dare step back into that fire."

Because I know exactly what it costs to walk away. "Boy, don't you dare step back into that fire."

I say it to the younger me. To the wounded me. To the part of me that still hears the streets calling, still feels the heat of the chaos that once made me feel alive—because the pain was the only pulse I knew. That fire, it made me. But it almost unmade me, too. It burned through everything I thought I was—my joy, my innocence, my right to dream.

And walking away wasn't brave in the way people imagined it. It wasn't bold. It wasn't loud. It was quiet.

It was trembling. It was lonely as hell. Because when you grow up in survival mode, peace feels like a trick. Love feels dangerous. And safety, you don't even recognize it when you find it. You flinch from it, distrust it, push it away before it can leave you like everything else did, I fought battles no one could see. Silent wars that played out behind my eyes. The kind of pain you don't name out loud because no one ever gave you the language. The kind that lives in your muscles, your heartbeat, your breath—and tells you to stay ready, stay guarded, stay hard.

Because softness was punished. Because feeling meant risk. Because vulnerability could get you killed. But healing—real healing—isn't about pretending it didn't happen. It's about learning to hold what happened without letting it hold you hostage. I've cried for the boy I used to be. The one who didn't get to be a child. The one who learned to walk like a man with wounds still open under his skin. The one who thought love had to hurt because that's all he saw growing up. And I've learned to say to him now—with gentleness, with compassion: *You did what you had to do to survive.* But now, you don't have to survive anymore. Now, you get to live. I am not the fight. I am not the fury. I am not the fire. I am the man who chose something harder. I chose healing. I chose softness without shame. I chose peace, not because I was tired—but because I was finally ready. Ready to feel. Ready to grieve. Ready to forgive. Ready to live a life that wasn't built around defense—but around truth. And now, I guard that peace like sacred ground. So, when the fire calls me back when the ghosts of the streets whisper like old friends, I say it again, louder this time, more certain:

"Boy, don't you dare step back into that fire."

Because you've come too far. You've felt too much. You've earned this life. And your story isn't about how close you came to burning— it's about how you rose from the ash.

Healing

I am steady now. Not because the storms stopped. Not because life has gotten soft or simple. But because I got intentional. Because I finally stopped letting chaos set the pace for my life. I built a peace that doesn't need to shout to prove it's real. A calm that doesn't shake every time the past knocks on the door. A strength that no longer swings back— because true power isn't always loud or violent. Sometimes, it's the quiet courage to stay grounded when everything in you wants to run. So no—I don't answer that old name when it's thrown like a test. I don't shrink to fit who I used to be, just to make others comfortable. I don't return fire just to feel alive. Not anymore.

I am not who I was.

But I don't hate him. I don't deny him. That boy—the one who fought to survive, I honor him. Because he made it through nights that should've broken him. He carried pain no child should carry. He protected me the only way he knew how—with fists, with silence, with rage disguised as power. That boy saved my life. But this man, this man is finally learning how to live it. To breathe without fear. To cry without shame. To speak without violence. To love without armor. Healing isn't forgetting. It's remembering without crumbling. It's facing the past without becoming it again. And now, when I look in the mirror, I see someone I'm proud of. Not because he's perfect— but because he chose the harder road. The one where peace is earned, where softness is strength, and where the journey isn't about escaping the fire—but becoming the light.

Holding the Line:

But I won't. I breathe. Deeply. Slowly. The way I do when I'm guiding someone through their own storm — the same way I ground my clients when they're on the edge of unraveling, when the past threatens to pull them under. I close my eyes, drawing the world inward, shutting out the noise. I place a hand over my chest, feeling the steady rhythm of my heartbeat — a reminder that I am still here. Still breathing. Still standing. And in that quiet moment, I whisper to myself, gentle but fierce: "Boy, don't you dare let him back out." Because I remember — oh, how deeply I remember — what it cost me to walk away from that old life. I remember the weight of the world pressing down on my shoulders, the heavy cloak of survival I carried for so long. The burden of leaving behind pieces of myself I thought needed to live, but that only chained me tighter. I remember the demons — the anger, the pain, the fear — wrestling inside me, sometimes screaming for release. I remember the tears I swallowed in silence, the nights when hope felt like a distant whisper and the loneliness that threatened to consume me. I remember the moments I wanted to give up — to sink back into the chaos because it was the only life I knew. And still, I chose to rise. So I will not go back. Not for memory, because the past is a place I honor but no longer live in. Not for ego, because proving anything to anyone means less than staying true to who I am becoming. Not for anyone, because my peace is mine to keep. This line — the one I hold — it's more than a boundary. It's a promise to myself. A promise that no matter how loud the past calls, no matter how strong the pull, I will protect the man I've fought so hard to be. I am not who I was. I am who I choose to be. And that choice is sacred.

The Names I Chose:

I am going by Andre now. Some call me Latif. These names aren't just words or labels tossed around to replace what came before. They are declarations — bold, intentional, and full of meaning. They are names I reached for with trembling hands and a hopeful heart, names I carefully chose in the quiet moments when I was rebuilding myself from the fragments of a broken past. They are not names the world handed to me without my consent — no, these are names born from healing, from reclaiming, from the fierce determination to rewrite my story. They carry the weight of intention, of growth, of transformation. They hold space for the man I am becoming — not just the shell I had to survive in the chaos, not the version of me forged in fear and fight. Andre, Latif — these names are the armor I wear now, but they're softer, warmer, gentler armor. Armor made of truth, compassion, and courage to be vulnerable. When someone speaks these names, they speak of the future I am building, the peace I am nurturing, the strength found not in battle but in becoming whole. These names are my promise to myself — a reminder that I am not bound by my past. That I am not defined by the pain I've endured. I am defined by the love I'm learning to hold for myself, the grace I'm growing into, and the healing I'm choosing every single day. And with these names, I stand tall. Not because I have forgotten where I came from but because I refuse to be a prisoner of it any longer. I am more than survival. I am life. I am becoming.

Those Still in the Dark Room

This story, it isn't just mine. It's ours —if you've ever found yourself perched on the edge of a bed at 3:17 a.m., the room dim, the silence thick, your thoughts louder than the city ever were. If your heart has ever felt too swollen with aches to fit inside your chest, then you know: this is for you. This is for those who stare at cracked ceilings and blank walls, not haunted by ghosts but by the echoes of memory —memories that don't knock; they barge in, loud as sirens, familiar as your own breath. The kind that loops like scratched records, asking questions with no intention of offering answers. This is for the ones who learned to smile through downpours because no one ever came with an umbrella. Who carry laughter like a shield — polished, rehearsed —not because they're fine, but because the alternative was unraveling in public. For those who confused survival with peace — because making it out becomes the victory, even if the war still rages behind your eyes. This is for those taught that silence was safer than softness, that to be loud was to be marked, and to be soft was to bleed in front of those who would never hand you a bandage. For the ones who grew up with sirens as lullabies and trauma stitched into the architecture of home. To the ones who believe healing is some distant, mythical thing — a word passed around in rooms you've never been invited to, spoken by people who never had to choose between groceries and grief, who never had to learn how to live while constantly preparing to die. To those who carry their pain in silence, who treat vulnerability like a luxury they can't afford, who equate softness with weakness, and surrender with shame — I see you. You're not broken. You're bearing weight no one was built to carry alone. And even in the dark room, you are not alone.

I Need You to Hear This

I need you to hear this —really hear it: Healing is not a lie. It's not some fairy tale sold in self-help slogans. It's not a luxury reserved for the privileged, the soft-spoken, or the lucky ones who never had to fight for breath. It's not a trend. Not a product. Not something you earn by being good, quiet, or clean. Healing is real. Messy, painful, holy, hard — but real. It doesn't always look like what you expect. It's not a perfect Instagram moment. It's not a yoga pose or a mantra whispered into candlelight —though sometimes, it's those things, too. But most of the time healing looks like waking up and choosing to keep going, even when everything in you says, "It's safer to stay numb." It looks like gritting your teeth through therapy. Like crying on the floor when no one's watching. Like saying "no" for the first time and "yes" to something that scares the hell out of you because it might actually be good. Healing is relearning your worth after a world convinces you that you never had any. It's holding your younger self with tenderness instead of shame. It's unlearning the belief that you are too far gone, too damaged, too broken to begin again. You're not. If you come from pain—the kind that sinks into your bones, that teaches you silence, that confuses love with fear, then healing isn't just possible. It's yours, too. It belongs to the weary, the wild, the wounded. To those who fought just to stay alive. To those who never had a roadmap but found the courage to search for something more. So let me say it again, louder this time: Healing is not a lie. It's not a trick. It's a birthright. And you—right now, as you are—are worthy of it.

HEALING IS A DECISION

(And Sometimes, It Hurts Like Hell)

Healing isn't pretty. It's not soft, light and gentle mornings. It's not a neatly folded blanket, a quiet journal entry or some curated, Instagrammable version of growth. Healing is brutal. It's messy. It's ripping the stitches out before the wound has finished bleeding because you finally realize what was sewn shut wasn't healing you; it was hiding you.

It's waking up in the middle of the night, heart racing, tears already falling, and having no idea why. Healing is standing in the wreckage of your life, your childhood, your relationships, your broken patterns— and realizing: *No one is coming to save me. It has to be me.* It's the rage that builds when you look back and see just how long you lived in survival mode. How long have you confused numbness for peace. How long you accepted silence as safety. You don't stumble into healing. You choose it. And that choice is violent, terrifying, and holy. Because healing demands confrontation. Of your past. Of your pain.

Of the parts of yourself, you swore you'd never speak out loud. It demands that you stop lying to yourself. That you stop minimizing what happened. That you stop pretending it didn't hurt just because you survived it. Healing means going back into the memories that still make your stomach turn. It means naming what was done to you without flinching. It means letting go of the fantasy that if you had just been better, quieter, easier to love—none of it would've happened. It means facing the truth: *It was never your fault.* And still—it became your responsibility to carry.

Until now. Healing is a decision. And some days, it feels like self-betrayal. Because you're letting go of the armor that protected you. The rage that kept you safe. The story you told yourself about being "fine" because admitting you were hurt felt like admitting defeat. But you are not defeated. You are rising. Even if your hands are still shaking. Even if your heart is still cracked open. Sometimes, healing looks like screaming into your pillow. Like cutting ties with people who once felt like home. Like grieving the version of yourself who only knew how to survive by shrinking, by pleasing, by disappearing. Like standing in front of the mirror and whispering, *"I'm still here."* Healing doesn't always feel like freedom. Sometimes, it feels like grief. Like dying and being reborn, again and again, in the same skin. But with every breath, every choice, every boundary—you're rewriting your story. And you don't owe anyone a polished version of your pain. You don't have to be graceful. You just have to be honest. You just have to be here. Because even now— even in your confusion, your chaos, your quiet breakdowns that no one sees—you are healing. You are unlearning. You are becoming. And to the part of you that still believes you are too broken, too far gone, too damaged to be loved, listen to me: You are not beyond saving. You are not the worst thing that ever happened to you. You are not a burden. You are a survivor of things most people will never understand. And that survival deserves to be honored, not hidden. This is what healing looks like. Not perfect. Not linear. Not easy.

But real. And real is enough. You are enough. Right here. Even in the wreckage. Even when it still hurts. You. Are. Becoming.

You Are Not Lost

(A Letter to the One Who's Still Trying to Find Their Way Home)

You are not lost. Even if it feels like you've been wandering for years. Even if the places that were supposed to be safe weren't. Even if every direction pointed you back to pain. Even if you had no map— just instincts, trauma, and whatever fragments of love you could carry in your clenched hands. Even if you were taught that survival was your only option, that vulnerability was danger, that silence was safety. Even if your body still wakes up in fight mode, still flinches at sudden kindness, you still don't trust peace when it finally shows up—you are not lost. You were navigating a storm no one else could see. You were building a home from rubble, carrying grief in your bones while smiling to make others comfortable. You were doing what no child should've had to do—protecting yourself.

Long before you had language for why it hurt. You are not too far gone. Not too broken. Not too late. You are not what they did to you. Not the chaos you adapted to. Not the mistakes you made when you were only trying to survive. You are not defective because your heart beats with caution. You are not unlovable because your softness got buried under years of armor.

The truth is: You adapted in ways no one taught you. You learned how to scan the room before taking up space. You learned how to stay quiet when your voice was never protected. You learned how to anticipate the mood in the house before you even stepped through the door. And maybe now, it's hard to let that go. Because sometimes, even pain feels familiar. Even exhaustion can feel like home. But listen—There is nothing wrong with you. There never was. You were responding to a world that made you unsafe. You were surviving what no one acknowledged. And you are still here. Still breathing. Still trying.

That alone is a miracle. You don't owe anyone your pain, your story, your breakdowns, your behind-the-scenes. You don't have to perform your past to be worthy of your present.

You don't have to prove that you suffered enough to deserve joy. You don't have to shrink yourself to be easier to understand. You don't have to stay angry to be taken seriously.

You don't have to keep carrying guilt for the ways you coped. Yes—there are things you've done that you're not proud of. But shame is not your home anymore. You are allowed to outgrow the version of yourself that only knew how to survive. You are allowed to be gentle. To be soft. To rest. To laugh again. Let me say this slowly and with everything I have in me:

You deserve peace. Not after you fix everything. Not after you forgive everyone. Not after you explain your whole life to people who never listened in the first place. You deserve peace now. In the middle of the mess. In the middle of the healing. In the space between breakdown and breakthrough. You are allowed to build a life that doesn't revolve around managing crises. You are allowed to leave people, places, and patterns behind—even if they once felt like family. You are allowed to stop proving, explaining, and apologizing. You don't owe your past a permanent seat at your table. You are not here just to survive anymore.

You are not here to keep rehearsing your pain for the approval of people who only stayed for the performance. You're here to live. To feel joy that doesn't come with a warning label. To wake up and feel safe in your own skin. To belong to yourself first, before anyone else. And if someone cannot sit with your peace without trying to break it, if they only value your pain because it makes them feel needed, let them go. You don't need anyone who confuses your healing with betrayal. Because you are becoming. Not better. Not perfect. But whole. Your softness is not weakness—it is your return. Your boundaries are not bitterness—they are a declaration: I will not abandon myself to be accepted. You are not lost. You are learning how to stay. Learning how to breathe when no one's watching. Learning how to be seen without flinching. Learning how to stop fighting yourself and start trusting the quiet. This is not the end of your story. This is the chapter where you come back home to yourself. Fully. Fiercely. Softly. On your own terms. And that is power.

I Left That Life Behind

(A Love Letter to the Self I Had to Outgrow)

I left that life behind. Not because I hated it. Not because I was suddenly strong enough. Not because it was easy. I left because it was never mine to keep. Because no matter how long I lived there—it never felt like home. That life was survival. Not living. It was built from broken things—and while broken things can be beautiful, they cannot always hold the weight of who you are becoming. That life knew how to endure. It knew how to pretend. It knew how to keep smiling through gritted teeth, how to laugh at pain just loud enough so no one could hear you cry. But it didn't know how to rest. It didn't know how to trust softness. It didn't know how to receive love without suspicion. I didn't walk away in triumph. I walked away with bloodied feet, my heart pounding like a warning bell in my chest, my hands still shaking from everything I'd carried for far too long. I didn't walk away because I felt ready—I walked away because I finally knew I deserved more. Not because I stopped hurting but because I stopped mistaking pain for proof of love. I stopped confusing chaos with the connection.

I stopped apologizing for wanting peace. Now, I am building something sacred. Not flashy. Not perfect. Not clean or curated. But honest. Whole. Free. I don't tell this story to glorify who I used to be. Not the anger.

Not the cold stare. Not the survival-mode reflexes I wore like a uniform. I tell it to honor the shift. To mark the turning point. To trace the thread of light that led me out. To say—I made it. Even if the map was missing. Even if no one clapped. Even if the only witness to my survival was me. Because of this wholeness you see it was fought for. Bled for. Wept over. Earned in the kind of battle no one else ever saw—the one inside. So if you're still there—in the dark room, on the floor, holding the pieces and wondering if they'll ever fit together again—listen to me. You are not weak because you're tired. You are not broken because you still feel the pull to go back. You are not failing just because healing hasn't happened fast. You are human. And you are trying. That is holy work. I know what it's like to wake up and feel like the air is heavy with ghosts. To carry stories in your body that you've never said out loud. To look in the mirror and not recognize the reflection—not because you don't see yourself, but because you've spent so long being who others needed, you forgot who you were allowed to be. But let me tell you this: You are not the worst thing that ever happened to you. You are not just a reaction to someone else's wounds. You are not doomed to repeat what you came from. You are allowed to become someone entirely new. And the light you're waiting for is not at the finish line. It's not at the end of your pain. It's not reserved for the "healed" version of you. The light is here.

Now. In every brave breath. In every boundary, you didn't apologize for. In every night you chose to stay. The light is in the moment you reach for help, even if your voice shakes. It's in the decision to rest, to cry, to say, "I matter," even when your mind tells you otherwise. The light is in every slow, silent step forward—the kind no one claps for. The kind that doesn't feel like a victory. The kind that just barely keeps you going. That is still light. You don't need to perform your pain. You don't need to stay broken just to be relatable. You don't need to bleed just to be believed. You are allowed to leave the fire—and never go back to prove you still can burn. You are allowed to be soft now. To be safe now. To be seen now. And you don't owe anyone a return to your wreckage. Not to explain. Not to justify. Not to make them more comfortable with your healing.

This version of you, the one who chooses to live—not just survive—The one who feels things deeply, who sets boundaries without shame, who speaks softly but stands firmly—That version of you is not a betrayal of your past. That version is the reward. The arrival. The reclamation.

And if no one ever told you this before—I would. You deserve to be here. Not just alive. But whole. Not just functioning. But free. Not just rebuilding. But reclaiming your joy. So keep going. Even when the progress feels invisible. Even when no one notices. Even when you feel like you're walking alone. You are not alone. And when you're ready—we'll be here. Not to fix you. Not to judge you. But to welcome you home. Because you were never lost. You were just becoming. Now you're almost home.

Chapter Five
Navigating Trauma and Identity

Let me say this from my chest: I don't run from *Jim Hart*. I don't curse his name or pretend he didn't exist. I couldn't — even if I wanted to. Because *Jim* isn't just someone I used to be. He's the reason I'm still alive. He carried me through storms no child should ever face taught me how to walk through fire without turning to ash. *Jim Hart* was the boy who never had time to be a boy. He was armor in human form a clenched jaw, a watchful eye, a voice always ready to bark before it broke. He knew what it meant to survive when the world around you didn't flinch at your suffering. And I honor him for that. But let's not romanticize him either. Because carrying *Jim Hart* isn't just about strength. It's about the *weight* of it — the ache, the grief, the ghosts. It isn't just a memory.

It's a wound that sometimes feels too fresh to touch. It's a door that still creaks open when I hear it, bringing in winds I thought I'd sealed out years ago. There are days I hear someone call it out — *"Jim!"* —and it's like my nervous system resets to survival mode. Shoulders tense. Jaw locks. My eyes scan the room like I'm back in my hood, Lexington Terrace, like I'm twelve years old again, trying to figure out if today is the day I get tested. Because that name… it doesn't always come with kindness. Sometimes it's a test. Sometimes it's a trap. Sometimes, it's a whisper from the past trying to pull me back into shoes that no longer fit but still feel familiar. I remember what it felt like to walk into those projects for the first time. Like stepping into a jungle where no one gave you a map, just eyes watching you, waiting to see if you'd break. Some kids offered friendship. Others offered fists. And I had to learn, fast:

Don't blink. Don't flinch. Don't show softness.

Softness was blood in the water. And I wasn't trying to bleed. Jim Hart was the boy who figured out how to survive. Stand tall, even when your legs are shaking. Speak with force, even when your voice is unsteady. Fight, even when all you want is for someone to hold you and say you're safe. That's the part people don't see. Not just the violence I witnessed but the love I needed and rarely received. The comfort I wanted but never asked for. The long nights I spent staring at the ceiling, thinking about everything I did wrong. Every loss. Every insult. Every name that slowly rewrote who I thought I was. Shame has a way of hiding in your bones and making a home there. And then there's that one memory. I was six. Holding my mother's hand. We walked into Woolworth's. I didn't want anything big—just a hot dog and a Coke. Something simple. Something a kid should be able to want without it turning into a lesson. But then we were told, "You can't sit here." No reason. No explanation. Just a cold look, a colder voice, and a refusal that felt like a door slamming shut. I didn't understand what I had done wrong. But my mother did. She held my hand tighter and said, "Come on, baby." Her voice cracked a little when she said it. Just enough for me to notice, even at six. I didn't understand that crack until years later. I thought she was just tired. But now I know it was something else. That moment wasn't about the food. It was about the message. About being told you don't belong. Being reminded, without words, that there are rules you don't get to break, no matter how young or how innocent you are. My mother's voice cracked because she couldn't protect me from that. She had lived it before. And she knew I'd live it again. And that's when I started learning the rules. Don't blink. Don't flinch. Don't let them see you hurt. Don't show them softness because they'll use it against you.

But what I didn't realize until much later is this: That kind of survival has a cost. You start to believe your armor is your identity. You forget that wanting peace isn't weakness. You stop asking for love because you're too used to fighting for space. I'm still learning how to unlearn that. Because the truth is, softness wasn't the danger. The danger was growing up thinking you had to live without it.

This world will not always see your humanity.

Fast forward a few years. I'm standing by the window on the eleventh floor, looking down on a street soaked in blood. Seven bodies. No sirens. No screaming. Just silence. That eerie kind of calm that comes when death stops shocking you. When it becomes something you recognize, I didn't cry. I didn't scream. I didn't even blink. By then, I had already learned how to go numb. It was the only way to keep breathing. That's the legacy Jim Hart carries. Not just survival. Not just strength. But trauma—deep, cellular, ancestral trauma. The kind that doesn't always announce itself but lives in your body. Passed down like an unwanted inheritance. It shows up in your posture. In your silence. In your instinct to always be on alert, even in rooms that feel safe. Even when there's no threat in sight. And that's why I had to claim my other name—the one I chose. Not to erase Jim. But to grow beyond him. I am Andre. I became Latif. Those names weren't given in fear. They were chosen in healing. They were born in therapy rooms, in prayer, in the quiet spaces where I finally let myself feel. They were shaped by people who didn't just see the damage—but saw the man underneath it. The one still possible. The one still worthy. So, when someone calls out, *"Jim!"*—I pause. I breathe. I ground myself. And I remind that boy inside me: *You're safe now. You don't have to fight anymore.* Jim Hart was never a failure. He was a fighter. And he still is. But I don't need to live in a war zone to prove I deserve peace. I don't need to keep bleeding to be believed. That name—Jim—is part of my story. But it's not the end of it. Because I'm still writing. Still healing. Still becoming. And today, I walked in the names I chose. Names that don't feel like defense. Names that feel like a release. Names that feel like home.

Chapter Six
Urban Trauma and the Fight for Healing

Urban trauma isn't just a series of violent events or isolated moments of crisis — it's a chronic, often invisible weight that entire communities carry. It's generational. Inherited. A legacy of pain handed down not just through genetics but through experience, environment, and the endless work of survival. It roots itself in the soil of systemic injustice — in neighborhoods shaped by redlining, policed by inequality, and starved of opportunity. It grows in homes where survival overshadows childhood, where grief is commonplace, and joy feels dangerous. It manifests in bodies like a hidden wound, reshaping how people move through the world — how they trust, how they speak, how they protect themselves. This trauma doesn't always look like someone curled up crying. Sometimes, it looks like hypervigilance. Like a child who's grown too soon. Like a teenager who strikes first because they never get the chance to strike last. Like a man who can't fall asleep in silence because silence has always meant something bad is coming.

That's like that twelve-year-old kid who hasn't slept through the night since his older brother was shot in front of their building. Teachers call him "disruptive." They don't see that he's grieving. That his outbursts are a language. That every slammed desk and shouted word is a shield built from fear. And that twelve-year-old teen is not alone. He's one of thousands — millions — who carry trauma that no one ever helped them name.

Research confirms what lived experience has long made clear: people in urban environments, especially Black and Brown communities, experience trauma at disproportionate rates. Not by accident — by design. This is the aftermath of structural racism: chronic exposure to violence, generational poverty, underfunded schools, over-policed neighborhoods, and healthcare systems that rarely see the whole person.

According to recent studies, children living in high-violence urban neighborhoods are diagnosed with PTSD at rates comparable to veterans returning from war. That statistic isn't just shocking — it's a siren. A call to understand that this isn't about individual failure. It's about systemic harm.

The result: Higher rates of anxiety, depression, and PTSD. Increased risks of substance use, heart disease, and early death. Not because these communities are weak. But because they've been holding too much, for too long, with too little support. They aren't broken — they've been broken down. And still, they survive. Still, they resist. Urban trauma reshapes identity. It teaches people that being hard is safer than being human. That softness is a liability. That silence is protection. That trust is a luxury. It distorts the meaning of strength until strength looks like numbness. Until feeling anything at all feels like a risk. But here's the truth: the people in these communities are not just surviving trauma — they are resisting it. Every day. With art. With laughter. With hustle. With care. With a brilliance that grows in cracked concrete. What's missing is not resilience — it's safety. It's systems that care. It's communities that heal. To understand urban trauma is to stop asking, *"What's wrong with them?"* and start asking, *"What happened to them?"* It's choosing to see beyond behavior and into pain. It's realizing that healing will never come through judgment — only through empathy, equity, and sustained, intentional care.

Because urban trauma may begin in pain, but it doesn't have to end there. With truth-telling, with justice, with resources that affirm life instead of policing it — we can begin to write a new story. One rooted not just in survival, but in becoming whole.

The Emotional Weight of Triggers

Urban trauma may begin in pain, but it doesn't have to end there. It starts in silence, the kind that lingers after sirens fade and gunshots stop echoing. It begins with losses that never got funerals. With stories that no one wanted to hear. With children learning to duck before they learn to read. With mothers praying through cracked windows and busted locks. But pain isn't the end. With truth-telling. With systems that see and support. With communities rooted in care — *real care*, not pity — We can begin to rewrite the narrative. Not from brokenness. But from the raw, sacred labor of becoming whole. Still — Wholeness doesn't come wrapped in pretty language. It's not a quick fix. It's not a yoga mat or a journal prompt. Because healing doesn't erase what happened, it teaches us how to carry it without bleeding every time we move.

And sometimes, all it takes is a name to knock the wind out of you. Every time I hear "Jim," something stirs. Not just in my mind. But in my breath. In my bones. In the places I've hidden from myself. It's not just a name. It's a signal. A spark. A storm is moving fast, without warning. Sometimes, "Jim" feels like sunlight on my skin. The warmth of being seen.

The rare peace of knowing someone had my back when I didn't even have my own. But other times, it feels like ice. Like being six years old again, walking into a store, I wasn't welcome in. Like watching my mother's pride fracture with a quiet crack, no one else heard.

There's gratitude in the memory. Jim carried grit like armor. He taught us survival wasn't optional — it was inherited. He knew the streets didn't care about soft hearts or second chances. So he built walls. Taught us how to build ours. But gratitude doesn't cancel out pain.

Because "Jim" doesn't just pull on memories —It pulls on scars. It reopens chapters I closed too fast. It drags me back into the rooms I tried to forget. That's how trauma works. It doesn't knock. It kicks in the door. Triggers don't care that it's been years. They don't care that I've been to therapy. That I meditate. That I pray. They bypass logic and head straight for the nervous system. Suddenly, I'm tense. Breath short. Chest tight. Hands clenched. Fists remembering fights I haven't fought in years. My spirit flinching — before I even know why.

This isn't a weakness. This is the residue of trauma. The price of surviving environments that asked me to stay alert or die. It's old wounds casting long shadows. It's the body remembering what the mind has filed away. It's the need to escape with no clear exit. And I know I'm not alone in this.

There are so many of us who carry names, faces, and street corners That feel like both home and harm. There are songs we can't listen to. Rooms we can't walk into. Holidays we dread.

Laughter that feels like a betrayal. A joy that comes with guilt. So many of us flinch at echoes — Not because we're fragile, But because we were never given the space to heal without armor.

We were handed toughness instead of tenderness. Discipline instead of empathy. Punishment instead of understanding. And we wore it all — like we were supposed to. But we're not just our trauma. We are not just the violence we witnessed or survived. We are not just the mistakes we made while trying to cope. We are not just statistics. We are not just what happened to us.

We are here. Still. Breathing. Healing — even when it's messy. Even when it's slow. Even when some days all we do is *not collapse*. And *that* is resistance. *That* is power.

Because healing is not forgetting, it's remembering *differently*. It's reclaiming what tried to destroy you — and saying, "You don't get the final word." Healing is finding safety where there once was fear. It's finding softness again. It allows joy without apology. It's building systems that don't just *watch* us survive — but help us live. We need more than resilience. We need refuge. We need rest. We need relationships that hold space, not just stories. We need a policy that protects, not punishes. We need care that's constant — not conditional. Urban trauma may have started the story. But we get to write the ending. And that ending, it won't be written in brokenness But in becoming whole. Together.

Healing and Moving Forward

What I've come to believe—deeply, without hesitation or compromises that one of the greatest failures in how we engage with our young people is our inability to truly see trauma for what it is. We rush to judgment. We label defiance as disrespect, silence as disinterest or disengagement, and anger as rebellion deserving punishment. But beneath those behaviors—beneath the surface—is often a landscape of pain we rarely stop to explore.

A pain so deep, so raw that it shapes how a child moves through the world, how they protect themselves, how they speak without words. What if we asked instead: *What hurt lives behind that defiance? What loneliness or fear hides behind that silence? What desperation fuels that anger?* Too often, we don't. We label what we don't understand, paint survival as defiance, and mistake trauma's echoes for bad behavior. We punish the symptom—the outburst, the withdrawal, the "attitude"—without ever trying to reach the root. And in doing so, we push young people further into isolation, further into pain, further from the healing they so desperately need. Healing is not found in punishment.

It is not discovered in rigid rules or cold discipline. Healing begins with a different kind of seeing—a kind of awareness that breaks past surface judgments and listens with a full heart, not just trained ears. This is the kind of awareness that sits quietly with pain, without rushing to fix it, without trying to erase it. It holds space for the raw, messy truth— the grief, the fear, the anger, the shame that has nowhere else to go. It's the awareness that understands behavior as a language, the only language a wounded soul sometimes knows.

Behind every "problem child" is a story waiting to be heard. A story of survival, of resilience that looks like defiance, of strength hidden in silence, of wounds carried so quietly they seem invisible. To truly heal, we must slow down enough to listen. To create spaces where young people don't have to hide their pain, where they can be seen— not as broken, but as whole people trying to navigate an unsafe world. This kind of healing asks for patience. It demands compassion. It requires us to hold pain without judgment, to offer presence instead of punishment, to respond with understanding instead of anger. Healing isn't a neat, linear path. It's a winding, uneven journey— marked by setbacks, by moments of doubt, by days when survival feels like the only option. But healing also carries hope.

Hope that someone will see the child behind the behavior. Hope that someone will believe in their worth, even when the child struggles to believe it themselves. Hope that pain can transform—not erase— into power, that stories once buried can become songs of strength.

This is the work before us. Not just to manage behavior, not just to enforce rules, but to heal wounds so deep they shape lives. If we want to move forward, if we want to build communities where young people can truly thrive, we must start by changing how we see.

We must learn to recognize trauma for what it really is: not a label, not a burden, not a problem to fix, but a human experience that calls for empathy, patience, and love. Healing begins when someone chooses to see the child—not the behavior. When someone offers a hand—not a punishment. When someone holds space—not judgment. This is how we move forward. Together.

Chapter Seven
What They Never Taught Us
about Wholeness

The Weight We Carry, the Light We Choose

Trauma-informed care is not a strategy. It's not a checklist or a classroom tool. It's a lens. A language. A posture of the heart. It's how we enter a room—with our assumptions softened, our listening turned all the way up. It's knowing that silence can be sacred—or survival. That the student staring blankly at the floor might be holding back a tidal wave. That the adult who explodes over nothing may be trapped in a moment their body never escaped. Pain doesn't always announce itself. Sometimes, it looks like withdrawal. Like zoning out mid-sentence. Like crossed arms and "I don't care" masks—when deep down, they care too much and can't bear to show it. To be trauma-informed is to be truth-informed. It's to see beneath behavior and into a story. It's to know that many of us were raised on high alert. That vulnerability was dangerous. That trust was a risk that cost us more than we could afford. Some of us learned to fight before we learned to speak.

To run before we ever knew how to rest. To shut down before we could name what hurt.

This, too, is a kind of inheritance—the nervous system passed down from those who had no space to feel safe. So, when you ask me,

"Why are you so angry?" I need you to understand I was never just angry. I was grieving the childhood I didn't get to live. I was scared, and shame told me I wasn't allowed to admit it. I was defending myself from a world that too often mistook my wounds for weakness. I carried the weight of it all in silence. Until silence began to break me.

But here's the truth: we get to choose the light, too. Even when the weight is still heavy. We get to choose presence overreaction. Curiosity over judgment. Compassion over control. Healing isn't the erasure of pain—it's the honoring of it. It's being able to say: *Yes, I've been hardened by this world, but I'm learning how to soften without breaking. Yes, I've been hurt, but I will not pass that hurt forward.* This is the work. To recognize the armor we needed—and then slowly, bravely, begin to set it down.

To see the hurt in others and choose not to turn away. To meet pain with presence, anger with understanding, and despair with dignity. Because the weight we carry is real. But so is the light we choose. And every time we choose to see differently—to listen deeper, to stay softer, to love anyway—we're making the world a little safer. For them. For us. For whom we're still becoming.

The Difference Safety Makes

Safety is not just a locked door or a police patrol. It's not the absence of noise—it's the presence of peace. Real safety lives in the nervous system. It's that slow, almost unfamiliar moment when your body says, *"You're allowed to breathe now."* It's a feeling. A knowing. A release. But for so many of us, especially in cities stitched together by red lines and ruptures, safety was never a given—it was a luxury. Something other people inherited.

We were taught to stay ready. Not to relax, not to trust, not to hope too loudly. We carry that conditioning in our shoulders, in our spines, in our sleep. Even in silence, we brace. Because our bodies remember what the world wants us to forget. In trauma-informed spaces, the rules shift. You don't have to earn your worth here. You don't have to perform calmness just to be seen as human. These are the places that don't flinch at your pain. They make room for the rage beneath your quiet. They say: *"We see what you've survived. We honor how you're still standing."* Because sometimes what looks like disrespect is actually a child who's never been taught they're worth protecting. Sometimes the "problem student" is a soul begging not to be erased. Sometimes, the flat stare, the sharp tone, the slammed door—is grief with no safe place to land.

The Psychological Residue of Urban Trauma

There's a weight you carry when every sidewalk holds a memory. When the air itself feels tense with stories no one has ever written down. When you've seen people disappear without leaving the block. When you've learned how to spot danger in a glance, in silence, in the way someone walks too close behind you. That's what trauma does. It trains you to survive, not to live. To expect pain. To normalize chaos. You stop looking for softness because, too often, it turns to betrayal. You start believing calm is just the quiet before the next storm. And still—we keep going. We make jokes in the rubble. We laugh loud enough to feel human again. We become fluent in the language of loss but still find ways to write joy.

What Healing Really Looks Like

Healing is not beautiful. It's not neat. It's nights you can't sleep because the memories don't respect your bedtime. It's crying over something small because your body finally feels safe enough to fall apart. It's sitting with your anger instead of drinking it. It's choosing not to run, even when every part of you screams, *"Get out. Disappear. Shut down."* Healing is the moment you stop pretending you're fine and start asking, *"What do I need right now?"* Even if the answer is messy. Even if it scares you, some days I feel whole. Other days, I'm piecing myself together by memory, by muscle, by faith. But I've learned that healing isn't about erasing the pain. It's about not letting it make all the decisions. It's being able to say: *Yes, I've been hurt in places no one can see. Yes, I've lost things I can never name out loud.* But I'm still here. Still loving. Still learning how to rest, how to trust, how to stay. Still building something soft in a world that taught me to be hard.

Jim Hart: A Chapter, not a Definition

Jim Hart is still in the story. Not as the villain. Not as the hero. But as the boy who bore the weight when no one else could. He is in the back alleys of my memory, in the locked rooms I used to avoid, in the tightness in my chest when certain names are spoken or when a sudden noise reminds me that I still flinch without meaning to. He's there. In the decisions I made in desperation, the ones I thought would ruin me—but somehow kept me alive. He's in the stare that went cold, so

I wouldn't cry. In the voice that got loud because no one listened to the quiet. He's in the fists, metaphorical or not, that I learned to raise long before I learned how to ask for help. Jim Hart was never a mistake. He was a defense. A boundary. A name that said: *I'll hurt you before you hurt me. I'll disappear before you get close enough to leave.* He was the armor I needed when softness was dangerous. When the world said boys don't cry, and men don't break, even though I was already broken and didn't know it yet. He was the mask I wore when vulnerability felt like exposure. He carried my rage when I didn't yet know it was grief. He held my secrets when I was still too ashamed to speak to them. And for that—I honor him. But honor is not the same as surrendering. Gratitude is not the same as allegiance. Because Jim Hart, for all his strength, was built on fear. And I'm not living in fear anymore. He taught me survival, but I am learning how to live. He taught me how to run, but I'm learning how to stay. He taught me how to be tough, but I'm learning how to be whole. And wholeness—real wholeness—does not mean rejecting the past. It means facing it. Holding it. Naming it without shame.

Jim Hart is not my shame. He is not my final sentence. He is not my ceiling. He is a chapter.

Raw. Real. Necessary. A map of where I've been—but not the compass guiding where I'm going. Because now, I write with a different hand. One that trembles sometimes but keeps writing anyway. Now, I speak with a voice I didn't know I had—a voice that no longer asks for permission to be heard. A voice that says: *I am more than what I survived.* The name I carry now is the one I chose. Not one given out of trauma, but one grown in healing. This name is quieter. Softer. But don't mistake that for weakness. It takes more strength to be gentle in a world that tries to harden you. It takes more courage to forgive than to fight. Jim Hart protected me when I needed a warrior. But I don't need war anymore. I need peace. I need breath. I need rest. And he can rest now, too. He doesn't have to be on guard.

He doesn't have to keep watch. I've got me now. So this is where we part. Not in rejection but in release. Not in forgetting, but in choosing. Because healing isn't erasing who you were— it's learning to love who you had to be and still choosing who you want to become. And I have chosen. This is my voice. This is my name. This is my story. And this— this is the chapter where I become free.

I Am Not My Trauma

I am not my trauma. I carry it — yes — but I am not it. I have worn its weight and felt it echo through my bones, but I will not let it define my name. I am more than what I have survived. More than the silence, I was forced to swallow. More than the fists, the fears, and the nights I cried into a pillow, I outgrew too young. More than the systems that labeled me before they ever listened. More than the mugshots that captured my pain but never my truth. More than the numbers they assigned me, like a barcode —as if healing could be calculated in digits. I am not what was done to me. Not the betrayal. Not the abandonment. Not the violence, or the shame, or the grief I was told to get over. I am not the decisions I made when I was desperate to feel something — anything — other than invisible. I am the boy who fought to live in a world that kept trying to kill his hope. I am the man who still shows up, even when his past is loud, and his healing is quiet. I am a reclamation. Of power. Of presence. Of peace. I am what happens when a soul refuses to stay small. When a heart, shattered a thousand times, chooses to keep beating — softer, yes, but stronger. I have the courage to begin again. The faith to believe there is more than survival. The sacred defiance of becoming whole in a world that only taught me to break. They called me broken. But I call myself becoming. So, when they try to reduce me to a file, to a case, to a statistic, let them read this: I am not my trauma. I am what grew in the aftermath. I am the healing. I am the choice. I am the proof. I am still here. And I am not done.

This Is What Power Looks Like

Power isn't control. It's not the loudest voice in the room. It's not having the final word, the sharpest comeback, or the coldest silence. It's not building walls so high that no one can reach you, not even the parts of yourself that still need tending. Power is something quieter. Something deeper. It's the decision to keep your heart open even when the world has taught you to close it. It's choosing not to become what hurts you. It's refusing to pass down what was passed to you. Power is compassion. It's staying soft when life tries to make you hard. It's letting your empathy breathe even when you were raised on survival, not tenderness. It's offering kindness when all you've known is coldness or chaos—not because you owe it to anyone, but because you've learned it sets you free. Power is grace. Grace for the child in you who didn't know better. Grace for the adult still learning how to live without fighting everything and everyone. It's holding your own hand in the dark. It's speaking gently to yourself, especially on the days when the old voices get loud. This is what I know now. Truths I didn't grow up with. Truths I had to claw my way toward, truths I had to learn the hard way: That it takes more strength to stay than to run. More courage to feel than to be numb. More bravery to forgive—yourself, especially—than to fight forever. That boundaries are not walls. That vulnerability is not a weakness. That healing is not linear, and progress is not always visible. That joy is an act of rebellion. That rest is resistance, and softness is strength. That survival taught me how to armor up. But healing taught me how to let go. Because real power is not performance. It's presence. It's not dominance. It's dignity. It's not perfection. It's permission—to be whole, to be messy, to be real.

This is what power looks like:

It's crying without apology. It's telling the truth even when your voice shakes. It's walking away without burning everything down. It's choosing peace when anger would be easier.

It's being able to say: *"I'm still here. I'm still learning. I'm still loving myself through it."* That—That is power.

Can Be Maps, Not Chains

Scars are not proof of failure. They are not marks of shame. They are not life sentences carved into skin or soul. Scars can be maps. Not chains. They don't have to keep you bound to the pain that made them. They don't have to drag you backward—to the moment it broke, the night you fell apart, the version of you that barely made it through. No. Scars can point forward. They can show you where you've already walked through fire—and remind you that you didn't burn to ash. They can whisper, *"You've been here before. You know how to survive this.* "They can teach you how to navigate the next storm with more wisdom, more clarity, more courage than before. Because scars tell a story, yes—but they are not your whole story. They are one chapter. A necessary chapter. A raw, unflinching, painful page—but not the end of the book. Not the title. Not the closing line. You are still writing. Still becoming. Still choosing who you get to be beyond what tried to break you. So, trace your scars not with shame but with reverence. Because they are proof you've healed enough to keep moving. Proof that something tore—and mended. That something was lost—but not everything. This is not where the story ends. This is where the next chapter begins.

Tears Can Be Teachers, Not Threats

I used to feel ashamed of my tears. Every time they welled up, I fought them back hard. Not because I didn't feel, but because I thought feeling made me weak. Because somewhere along the way, I learned that crying meant losing control. That if I cried in front of someone, they'd think less of me. That my pain needed to stay hidden to be respected. So, I trained myself to be tough. I held everything in. Even when I was hurting. Even when I felt like I was drowning inside. Especially then. I thought silence was strength. That composure was maturity. That "holding it together" was the only acceptable response to pain. But what I've come to understand—slowly, painfully, over time—is that tears aren't the enemy. They're not evidence of failure or weakness. They're proof that something matters. That something inside of me is asking to be heard. To be felt. To be honored. Tears show up when something inside says, *"This hurts." "This mattered." "This needs space."* And that's not a weakness. That's honesty. Crying has taught me more about myself than almost anything else.

Because tears don't lie. They come when the weight gets too heavy to carry in silence. They show up when the emotions are too deep to name out loud when grief doesn't have words. When disappointment is still too fresh to talk about. When I feel unseen, unheard, or completely alone, there were moments I thought I had moved on— until a single tear reminded me I hadn't. Moments when I didn't even know I was carrying something until my body said, *"Here it is. Feel it."* Tears are the body's truth. They're the moment the heart speaks, even when the mouth can't. And I've learned that those moments matter. They are not signs that I'm falling apart. They're signs that I've been holding it together for too long. They're signs that I'm human that I care deeply. That I'm still open, even after everything.

Now, I don't rush to wipe them away. I don't apologize when they come. I let them fall because I know what they mean. They mean I'm showing up—for myself. They mean I'm not running anymore. They mean I'm strong enough to feel. Tears don't make me fragile. They don't make me less. They make me real. They remind me that I haven't gone numb. That I still feel love. Loss. Longing. That I still hope. And in a world that tells us to toughen up, to keep moving, to bury the pain—choosing to feel anyway is powerful. Tears don't break me. They help me breathe. They help me begin again. They help me remember I'm still here—and still healing.

Vulnerability Is Not Weakness

Vulnerability is not a weakness. It's not the absence of strength—it's the very beginning of it. True strength doesn't come from hiding behind walls or armor. It comes from the bravery to let those walls fall, to stand exposed in your uncertainty, your fears, and your imperfections.

Letting yourself be seen—not just at your best, but at your most fragile—that's courage.

It's showing up when your voice trembles, when your hands shake when the words feel like they might catch in your throat. It's speaking your truth even when it's uncomfortable, even when you're not sure how it will be received. That kind of courage isn't loud or flashy. It doesn't demand attention or applause. It's quiet. Steady. Deeply real. Vulnerability is not about falling apart or losing control. It's about opening. Opening your heart, your mind, your spirit—allowing yourself to be seen in all your messiness and beauty. It's the gateway to connection—to truly be seen and understood by others, to build bridges instead of walls. It's the gateway to healing—because healing needs space, and space needs openness. It's the gateway to becoming whole—to embracing all the parts of yourself, not just the polished, confident ones. If you are trying to grow, to heal, to stay open in a world that constantly tells you to close off, that resistance itself is power. If you are learning how to love yourself without conditions, without needing to earn it or prove it, that is power. If you show up anyway—even on days when you want to hide, even when it's hard, even when it feels like you have nothing left to give—that's power. This kind of power doesn't shout. It doesn't need to. It's quiet. It's earned through every small step forward, through every time you choose openness over protection, through every moment you hold space for yourself and others. And this power lasts. It carries you through the storms. It builds resilience that no hardship can erase. Vulnerability is not the absence of strength—it is the truest form of strength there is.

Still Becoming

Every day, I wake up still becoming. Still figuring things out. Still unlearning habits I picked up just to survive. Still remind myself that I don't have to be who the world told me I had to be. Still trying to write new endings to old stories that have lived in me for too long. Some days, I get it right. Some days, I don't. But I'm still here. And that counts for something. If you see me quiet, please don't assume something is wrong. Sometimes, I'm just thinking, resting, giving myself space to feel. Sometimes, silence is how I protect my peace.

It's how I process. It's how I heal. If you see me smiling, know it's not because life is perfect. It's because I've learned to find joy in the small things. To let myself feel light when it comes. Because for a long time, I didn't think I deserved it. And if you see me still—really still—know that's a big deal for me. Because for most of my life, I didn't know how to slow down. Stillness felt unsafe. It felt like a weakness. Now I know it's strength. It's a sign that I'm not constantly running anymore—from fear, from pain, from myself. Healing, for me, isn't about being "fixed." It's about learning to live honestly. It's about accepting where I've been while staying open to where I'm going. It's about choosing to show up—on the good days and the hard ones too. It's about staying when everything in me used to want to leave. It's about believing in a future I can't always see—but choosing it anyway. So yes, I'm still becoming. And I probably always will be. But for the first time, I'm okay with that.

Chapter Eight
Before We Had Words
for Healing

It wasn't just us.

The fear. The hypervigilance. The feeling of always being on edge, even in silence—these weren't personal flaws. They were symptoms of something deeper. A 1991 study from the *Archives of General Psychiatry* found that in a group of young adults from Detroit, over 39% had experienced traumatic events, and nearly 1 in 4 of them developed PTSD. That's not a coincidence; that's a crisis.

And the numbers don't even tell the full story. Because what about those of us who never got diagnosed? Who never saw a therapist? Who didn't have language for trauma, only reactions to it? What about the boys who flinched at kindness because they were taught softness would get them killed? Or the girls who became caregivers before they finished being children? We were living with wounds that had no bandages. And yet—we showed up. We survived. Some of us, like me, even found a way to heal.

We didn't call it trauma. We didn't have therapists or diagnoses or journals full of reflection. What we had was instinct, rhythm, and routine—coping mechanisms dressed up as ordinary life. Before we had words for healing, we had spaces that held us. We had elders who watched over us without saying much, music that steadied us, and fleeting moments of beauty that slipped through the cracks in our pain. We didn't talk about what hurt. We survived it. Silently. Together. Lexington Terrence Recreation Center wasn't just a building—it was the emotional scaffolding of our neighborhood. It stood like a steady pulse in a city block riddled with sirens, silence, and survival. It was our sanctuary, our secret shelter in plain sight. A place where joy wasn't just possible it was *practiced*. We didn't always understand what the Rec Center was giving us. We didn't know how to articulate what it meant to feel safe, held, or seen. But our bodies knew. Our nervous systems knew. It was sacred. It gave shape to our days, rhythm to our summers, and somewhere to lay down the emotional weight we were too young to name, too busy surviving to unpack. The world outside demanded we be tough, fast, and alert. But inside those walls, we could breathe. Play. Eat. Dance. Draw. Laugh. Cry, sometimes—not always aloud, but in a quiet way, children do when they don't yet know what grief is, only that it lives in their chest like a second heartbeat. Before we had language for healing, we had Lexington Terrence. And it was enough to keep us going.

. Daycare, Discipline, and Distraction

During the day, the Rec Center transformed into an informal daycare—a lifeline for working single parents, especially mothers, who handed off their children with the quiet hope that we'd be safe, fed, and seen. It wasn't officially licensed, maybe not even fully staffed by today's standards, but it offered something our homes and streets often couldn't: structure without fear. There were free lunches served with paper napkins and soft voices. Board games with missing pieces that still made us feel whole. Basketballs with more air than grip jump ropes that slapped the pavement like music. And then there were the arts and crafts tables where chaos met with color. Mr. Reynolds ran the center with quiet authority, the kind that didn't need to raise its voice. He knew every name, every sibling, every story. His presence alone settled the room. Mrs. Sharp was different, softer, slower, and deliberate in how she moved. She ran the arts and crafts room, a sacred little corner of the building where we weren't expected to be loud or, fast or tough. Just a present. Just kids. Her table was covered in glue sticks, safety scissors, beads, buttons, construction paper, and popsicle sticks—tools of temporary transformation. What looked like child's play was something deeper. We painted through pain. We stitched through stress. We glued things together while everything around us seemed to fall apart. We didn't know it at the time, but what we were doing was therapy in disguise. We were learning how to focus, how to make decisions, and how to finish something. We were learning emotional regulation through construction paper and glitter. In those moments, we weren't poor. We weren't scared. We weren't leftovers of a system built to forget us. We were creators. Builders. Artists of our own small world. And even if we left those projects behind when the doors closed, something inside us has some capacity to cope, to calm, to imagine staying with us long after.

Summers of Sound and Sanctuary

Every summer, Operation Champ rolled into our neighborhood like a caravan of joy, a parade of possibility. The bounce of the trampoline, the thump of bass from the speakers, the smell of hotdogs riding the thick summer air—suddenly, the block wasn't just a block. It was a celebration. A place transformed, if only for the afternoon. For a few radiant hours, we weren't poor. We weren't worried. We weren't watching windows, dodging tension, or learning how to read the room before we entered it. We were just kids—laughing, breathless, sticky with sun and snow cones, spinning beneath a sky that, for once, didn't feel so heavy. But beneath all that brightness lived something unspoken. Urban trauma isn't just the violence you see; it's the silence it leaves behind. It's in the way we flinched at loud sounds. The way we always checked behind us. The way our fun was frantic as if joy might vanish at any moment—because it usually did. Operation Champ didn't erase the trauma, but it interrupted it. It carved out moments of levity in the middle of emotional war zones. It gave our nervous systems a break and taught our bodies—however briefly— that joy was not only possible, it was *allowed.* And that was no small thing. And then there was Camp Concern. Camp Concern, let us leave. Not just the city but the state of hypervigilance we didn't even know we lived in. For a few days each summer, we swapped the constant alerts of survival for trees, cabins, and counselors who looked us in the eye and asked, *"How are you?"*—and meant it. It was there, outside the city's concrete shell, that many of us experienced the absence of fear for the first time. No sirens. No street codes. No pressure to posture.

Just stars, space, and the strange permission to feel safe. What we couldn't articulate back then but understand now is that these experiences weren't just fun—they were trauma interventions in disguise. Structured joy. Scheduled release. Small doses of peace to soothe bodies locked in fight-or-flight. We didn't know it, but we were being taught to imagine a life beyond survival. To feel something other than numb. To dream beyond our borders. It wasn't therapy in the clinical sense. But it was healing—quiet, slow, intentional. And in neighborhoods where trauma was inherited like a surname, that kind of healing was radical.

Talent Shows and Unspoken Therapy

The Lexington Terrence talent shows were the crown jewels of our calendar. When they happened, the whole block felt brighter, louder, and more alive. Families packed into the rec center like it was revival night. Aunties in their Sunday best, cousins crowding the front row, toddlers on laps, and elders posted in the back—arms crossed, eyes soft. It wasn't just entertainment. It was a ceremony. I first reflected on those nights in *I Found a Way Out* (Hart, 2025), where I wrote that those nights gave us more than just joy—they gave us healing.

Kids sang, danced, recited poetry—some off-key, some off-beat, some so full of soul it made your chest ache. The applause came easy and loud, wrapping around each performer like a warm coat. No matter how small the act was, the crowd clapped like they were witnessing brilliance—because, in a way, they were. We laughed. We cried. We forgot—for a moment. What I didn't understand then— what I saw so clearly now—is that those nights weren't just events. They were rituals. Not ceremonial for tradition's sake but born from necessity. Strategic, intentional responses to the chronic stress and emotional fatigue we carried in our bones before we even knew the words for them. They were how we coped. How we processed what we couldn't name. In a community burdened by generational weight—

from the relentless grip of poverty, from the quiet violence of systemic neglect, from the invisible grief of daily survival—these talent shows and the energy around the recreation center were far from frivolous. They were lifelines. Anchors. Acts of resistance disguised as celebration. We didn't have wellness centers. We had the stage. We didn't have therapists. We had neighbors shouting our names from folding chairs. We didn't call it healing—but that's what it was. And this was not new. Ours was a lineage of survival stitched together through improvisation—finding ways to feel human in conditions designed to strip that away. Consider, for example, a different kind of lifeline—captured decades earlier in a moment of stillness and focus: Afro-American Newspapers/Gado/Getty Images. *African American Youth Playing Billiards at the Lexington Terrace Housing Project, Baltimore, Maryland, November 16, 1948.* Photograph. Getty Images. Even here, in this black-and-white image, you can sense it: the ritual of play, the quiet concentration, the creation of joy and order within chaos. The table wasn't just for billiards. It was a place to gather. To forget. To belong. Whether it was the flicker of a spotlight on a makeshift stage or the crack of a cue ball in a dimly lit rec room, these moments were survival. They were ours.

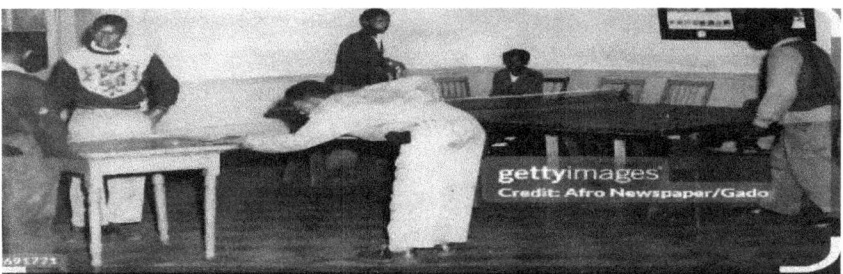

They allowed us to perform joy even when we didn't fully feel it. To rehearse pride even when the world gave us few reasons to. To practice being seen, loudly and unapologetically, in a society that often refused to acknowledge us at all.

And for kids like me, who didn't yet know what it meant to hold trauma in our bones, who just thought the knot in our stomach was "normal," these nights gave us something sacred: recognition. That nod from the crowd. That shout from a neighbor. At that moment when the lights hit your face and, for once, you didn't have to shrink. No therapist. No diagnosis. Just a mic, a beat, and a room full of people rooting for your light. Looking back, I realize those talent shows weren't just performances. They were therapy—coded in rhythm and claps. Healing—disguised as fun. Love—disguised as tradition. In communities starved for resources, joy became our medicine. And we passed it around like communion.

The Residue of Survival

What lingered—long after the last note of the music, long after the applause faded and the folding chairs were stacked—was something more complicated than nostalgia. Beneath the surface of those joyful memories lived the psychological residue of survival. The fear we carried. The grief we didn't speak. The trauma that shaped our sleep and tightened our shoulders before we even knew what tension was. We didn't have the language back then, but we lived the symptoms. Startle reflexes. Sleeplessness. Sudden silences. We laughed hard but trusted slowly. We moved fast, not just out of play but out of instinct.

Out of necessity. The Rec Center didn't erase that—it couldn't. But it gave us a place to carry it.

To hold the weight without being swallowed by it. To set it down, even temporarily, in rooms filled with music and movement and make-believe. It didn't fix everything. It couldn't stop what waited for us outside. But it helped us *manage*. It taught us how to *cope*. And most of all, it gave us reasons to *continue*. Long before we had names for our pain, we were developing tools to survive it. Not in clinics or classrooms—but through dance contests, talent shows, camp trips, and afternoons spent gluing glitter to paper hearts. In a system built to discard us, Lexington Terrence modeled something radical: That joy is not a luxury.

It is a discipline. A strategy. A lifeline braided from music, memory, and community care. We didn't just survive there. We rehearsed what it meant to be whole, which shaped our sleep. But the Rec Center gave us a place to hold that pain without being consumed by it. It didn't fix everything. But it helped us manage, cope, and continue. It gave us the tools to navigate trauma long before we knew how deeply it had shaped us. And most importantly, it modeled something radical in a broken system: that joy is not a luxury—it is a discipline, a strategy, and sometimes, a lifeline. Times New Roman

What the City Took, What the Center Gave

I didn't set out to write a memoir. I set out to remember—because so much of what shaped me was never written down. It lived in the cracks of sidewalks, in overheard conversations, in the echo of a basketball hitting concrete outside Lexington Terrence Recreation Center. This isn't just a story about one neighborhood. It's about what happens to people, especially children—when systems fail, when poverty becomes policy, and survival becomes culture. But it's also about what grows in the ruins. I write this not from a place of bitterness but from a place of balance. Grief taught me how to notice joy. Trauma taught me how to treasure softness. And the Lexington Terrence Rec Center taught me that even in broken places, healing has roots—quiet, steady, and sacred. This is for the ones who never got to tell their stories. This is for the ones still surviving, still shining. This is for the kids who grew up too fast—and found ways to hold onto the light.

The Quiet Return to Ourselves

(Some Places Never Leave You. Some Parts of You Wait to Come Home.)

Time moved on. Not with fanfare, not with fireworks. Just… silence. The kind that lingers long after the music stops. The Rec Center eventually closed—like so many places that once held us together when the world felt like it was coming apart. No breaking news. No final dance. No goodbye mural to say thank you. Just an empty building where a heartbeat used to be. Just dust where our laughter used to echo. And then people scattered. Some moved away—chasing jobs, chasing peace, chasing breath. Some never left— same faces on the same corners, still watching, still hoping the block might apologize for all it took. And some…some just disappeared.

Into addiction. Into anger. Into the systems that said we were too much, too loud, too broken.

Some into graves. Too many graves. And I left, too. More than once. Left with suitcases full of guilt. Came back with a quieter voice and heavier eyes. Left again—each time carrying something I didn't know how to name. But here's what I know now: You never really leave the places that shaped you. Not the streets. Not the stories. Not the rooms where your joy first learned to stretch. You carry them. Even when you think you've outgrown them. Even when you wish you could forget. I still carry the rhythm. The noise. The resilience. The way we made music out of scarcity. The way we clapped like we were calling each other back to life. The way we made pain into performance—not for applause, but because we didn't know another way to speak our truth. The Rec Center didn't fix us. It didn't heal the trauma we went home to. It didn't stop the evictions, the sirens, the ache of being young and unseen. But it did something else.

Something quiet. Something holy. It reminded us—maybe for the first time—that we were worth saving. That we were more than the damage. More than our defense mechanisms. More than the hard shells we wrapped around our hearts just to make it to tomorrow. I still feel the residue. Still, double-check the locks. Still flinching at fireworks. Still, scanning every room like an escape plan is part of the furniture. But now, I know why. Now, I don't shame myself for it. That's healing, too. Not forgetting—but remembering differently. Not just what hurt but what helped. Who helped. Who stayed. Who said, "I see you," even when we were hiding in plain sight.

There are things I'm still unlearning. Reflexes are born from fear. The way I raised my voice when I didn't feel heard. The way I shut down when it felt too dangerous to feel. But piece by piece, I'm coming home to myself. To the softness, I was told to kill. To the gentleness, I buried so deep I thought it had died. To the child who wanted more than survival—who wanted to feel safe. To be held. To belong. And now, I do belong. Not to a place but to people. To a version of myself that is whole, not because nothing broke, but because I put the pieces back together without shame.

We were never just surviving. We were inventing joy in the ruins. We were building a family out of strangers. We were practicing freedom with every laugh, every dance, every shouted lyric that drowned out the sirens outside. And now, finally, with the language we didn't have then— we can say what we couldn't say before: That love was real. That resilience was real. That we mattered, even when the world didn't see it. So, if you're still holding the weight of places that vanished before you were ready... If you're still carrying the sound of doors that never reopened... If you've left and returned, left and returned—not knowing where "home" begins or ends...This is for you. You are not forgotten. You are not alone. You are not just a memory of who you had to be. You are still here. Still becoming. Still allowed to come home—to yourself.

Because the quiet return to ourselves isn't loud. It isn't fast. But it is holy. And it is happening.

Right now. With every word. With every breath. With every time, you choose love over fear.

And the best part is we're doing it together.

Final Chapter:
The Journey Continues

I know what it means to be lost—not lost on a map but lost in yourself. I've moved through life with a painted-on smile, doing my best to look whole while inside, I was breaking. I've sat in crowded rooms feeling like I was drowning, screaming silently beneath the surface, unseen and unheard. The guilt, the shame—they weren't passing emotions. They were anchors. Weights tied to my ankles. Voices in my head whispering I didn't deserve another chance. That I was too far gone. That healing wasn't meant for people like me. But somehow, against all logic, all pressure, and all pain—I got back up. Not in a dramatic moment. Not in one big leap. But in pieces. Slowly. Quietly. Unevenly. Painfully. And let me say this plainly: getting back up is not beautiful. It's not cinematic. It's not the kind of comeback that people post online. It's crying until you shake, then wiping your face and showing up anyway. It's learning to live with the parts of you that once felt unlovable. It's sitting with your past without letting it sit on your chest. It's fighting to believe you're worthy—every single day.

Getting back up means forgiving yourself for things no one else even knows about.

It means breaking patterns that were never yours to begin with. It means growing in silence, without applause or recognition, just because you *have* to. The truth is the world rarely celebrates this kind of healing. It is like the before-and-after stories. The polished surface. The cleaned-up version. People want your redemption, not your process. They want the outcome, not the cost. They want to skip the middle. But I lived in the middle. I *am* in the middle.

And even if the world never sees the nights, I talked myself out of quitting, the days I carried grief like it was part of my skin, the mornings I got up when nothing in me wanted to—I see it. I know what it took. I remember who I was when I didn't think I'd survive. And I'm proud of that man. I'm proud of what he endured. Of what he chose to become. I'm proud of the way I rebuilt a life with hands that once only knew how to shake. I am proud of how I chose softness in a world that taught me to harden. Proud of how I stayed—when walking away would've been easier. Yes, some days, I still hear the echoes of who I used to be. I still carry the weight of memories that haven't fully faded. But I'm not hiding from them anymore. I face them. I carry them. I *own* them. Because they are not chains. There are *evidence* that I'm still here. And now, I fight for something different. I fight for peace. I fight for rest. I fight for a future that belongs to *me*— not to the version of me that broke, but the version that *chose* to rebuild. This isn't the end of my story. But it is the end of this chapter. The part where I was only surviving. The journey continues—but this time, I'm not running. I'm not proving. I'm *living*. Freely. Softly. Fiercely. On my own terms. And that is enough.

Final Dedication

To the version of me who almost didn't make it—the boy who carried more than any child ever should, who smiled through cracked teeth and called it strength, who mistook being needed for being loved and survival for identity. You were never weak. You were never broken. You were becoming. And to every soul who has ever sat in silence, wondering if they mattered—You do. I see you. I hear you. I believe in your becoming, too. You are not your wounds. You are not what happened to you. You are not the person others failed to protect. You are the evidence that healing is possible. That choosing yourself is a kind of revolution. That peace—honest, hard-earned peace—is not a myth. It's real. And it's yours to claim. This story was never just mine. It was always *ours*. So, if you're still here—still breathing, still becoming—thank you.

You Are the Reason I Wrote This

To the staff at the Lexington Terrace Recreation Center—Mr. Reynolds, Mrs. Sharp, and every soul behind Operation Champ and Camp Concern—thank you. Thank you for giving us joy we didn't yet understand was a form of therapy. For the games that weren't just fun but medicine. For the structure that felt like protection in a world that often felt like chaos.

For creating spaces where we could simply be—loud, awkward, goofy, free. You gave us the gift of childhood in a place that rarely made room for it. You gave us moments that turned into memories, memories that became lifelines. I carry your kindness with me still.

To the mentors, professors, counselors, and friends who met me as a grown man but still made space for the frightened child I kept hidden inside—your compassion gave me permission to unfold. You saw the parts of me I was still learning to name. You offered mirrors that reflected back not what I was but what I could be. You handed me language when all I had were wounds. You listened without judgment. You taught me that healing doesn't always happen in grand gestures—it happens in small, consistent acts of love and care.

To my readers—whether you've lived this pain, brushed up against it, or simply opened this book to understand someone else's story— thank you. Thank you for your curiosity, your empathy, and your willingness to sit in discomfort. Thank you for holding these pages with grace. Thank you for witnessing what was once too heavy to say out loud. You have walked with me through memories that once tried to define me. You reminded me that my story matters—not just for me, but for those still searching for language, still searching for hope.

And finally—**to God**. Thank you for never calling me back to the pain but always calling me forward into purpose. For staying close when I felt far. For sending people, moments, and mercy right on time. For whispering truth into the hollow places and reminding me I was never abandoned. I was being prepared. You are the reason I wrote this. Every broken part of me that dared to believe in wholeness. Every quiet voice that longed to be heard. Every reader still carrying something heavy. Every survivor is still learning how to rest. This book is for you. For us. For all the ways we're still becoming. With deep love, reverence, and gratitude.

Dear Readers,

First—**thank you**.

Thank you for picking up this book. Thank you for holding it in your hands, for opening it, for letting these words enter your world, even if just for a moment. Thank you for making space—not just for this story, but perhaps for your own.

Don't Call Me Back is more than a memoir. It's a mirror. A reckoning. A letter to the boy I used to be—and a love song to the man I've fought to become. It is a record of survival, yes, but also of rediscovery. It's the story of what happens when your first language is pain, but your heart dares to learn healing.

Writing this book was not easy. Some chapters were written with tears in my eyes, others with silence sitting heavy in the room. There were moments I wanted to walk away from it, from myself, from the memories that still throb like bruises. But I kept writing—because I knew someone needed this. Maybe you. Maybe the version of me who once felt invisible.

I wrote this for the ones who've been told to "man up" before they ever had a chance to be a child. For those who've been needed but never nurtured. For the ones labeled before they were loved. For the tired, the tough, and the tender-hearted who are still trying to make sense of what they carry. For those who have done the hard, soul-deep work of healing—and for those who are just beginning to whisper, *maybe I deserve peace too.*

Wherever you are on your journey, just starting, in the thick of it, or finding your breath on the other side, I want you to know your pain is valid. Your healing is holy. Your story is still unfolding. This book is not a neat ending. It is a beginning. It is not closure. It is clarity. It is not a victory march. It's a quiet act of faith. A trembling hand reaches toward the light.

If you find yourself in these pages, I hope you also find permission—to grieve, to grow, to forgive, to rest. To be soft in a world that tried to harden you. To be seen in the fullness of your truth. To be loved without performance. To take up space without apology. The trauma we inherit—be it generational, urban, or unspoken—does not get the final word. The scars we carry are not evidence of failure; they are maps, tracing where we've been and how far we've come. They are proof that we've survived what tried to silence us.

So if you're still here—still breathing, still becoming—I want you to know: You are not alone.

You are not what happened to you. You are not broken. You are *becoming*. You are allowed to evolve. You are allowed to rewrite the story. And you never—*never*—have to answer when the past tries to call you back.

With love, humility, and deepest gratitude,

Andre Hart

Acknowledgments

This book was never mine alone. It is woven from the lives, the wounds, and the resilience of countless others who walked beside me—sometimes silently, sometimes fiercely—through the shadows and light of a world that often feels unforgiving. To my mother and father, who carried the weight of a world that gave them little rest or mercy, your quiet love was my refuge. In the noise of streets that demanded toughness, you showed me strength through tenderness. Even when your own heart was breaking, you held space for mine. Thank you for teaching me that love doesn't always roar; sometimes, it simply stays. To the elders in my neighborhood, those invisible pillars, the unspoken guardians who held us in their gaze and their acts of care, who fed us when hunger was a constant companion, who offered protection without asking for thanks, who passed down survival not just as a skill but as a sacred inheritance—your presence was a lifeline. Your strength was a shield.

You taught me what it means to endure with grace, even when the world seemed bent on breaking us. To the children I grew up with, the unseen warriors of our neighborhoods— you who carried trauma before you had words for it, who navigated streets that taught us to be both hard and invisible, who learned to survive by reading between silences and stepping over scars—this story carries your names, your pain, and your hope between every line. Our shared history is written in wounds that never fully heal but also in the fierce beauty of our survival.

Urban trauma is more than a moment—it's a residue that settles deep in the bones, in the hesitation to trust, in the quickened heartbeat at a sudden sound, in the way silence can feel both like safety and suffocation. It is inherited pain, passed down like a shadow no one asked for, yet somehow, from this darkness, we find the fragile, stubborn roots of healing. To everyone who helped me navigate that terrain—whether through words, presence, or simply by holding space—this book is as much yours as it is mine. Thank you for being witnesses, for refusing to turn away, for believing in the possibility of light when all I saw was shadow.

Echoes of Support

To everyone who has purchased I Found a Way Out—

From the depths of my heart, thank you for supporting my first book, *I Found A Way Out.* Your support is more than a kind gesture — it's a lifeline. It tells me that stories of survival matter, that voices once silent can finally be heard, and that healing is not only possible but shared. By holding this book, you're not just reading my journey — you're standing beside me in it. You're witnessing the pain, the courage, the unraveling and rebuilding. And that kind of presence is sacred. Every page you read, every moment you reflect, is a quiet act of compassion — not just for me, but for yourself and others who may still be searching for a way out. You remind me why I wrote this, why I chose to speak when silence felt safer. And why I'll keep speaking — for those who can't, for those still trying. Thank you for walking this path with me, for choosing this book, and for carrying its message in your heart.

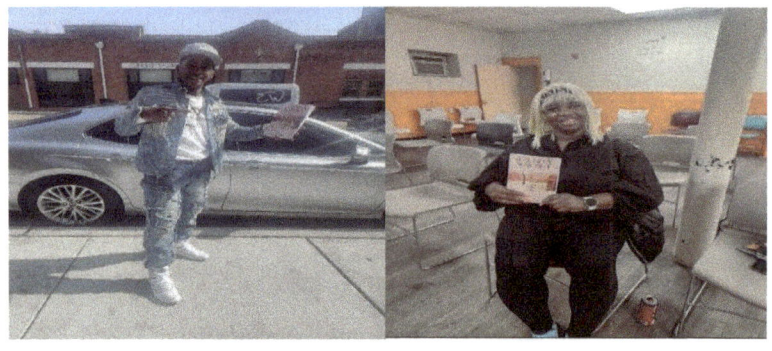

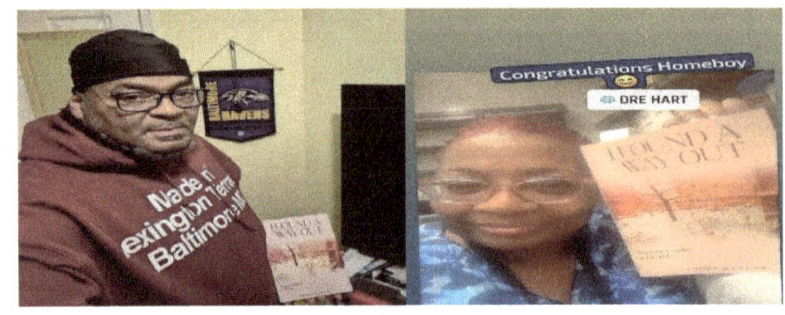

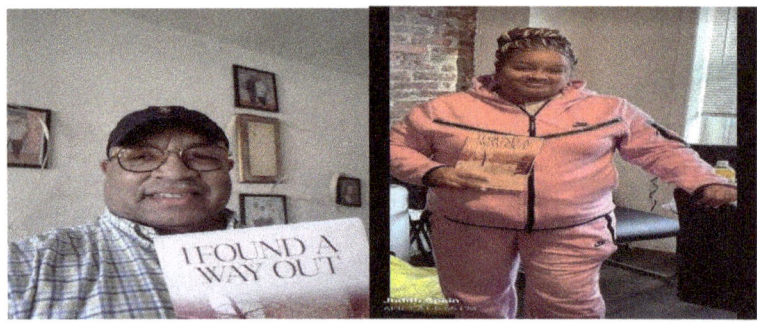

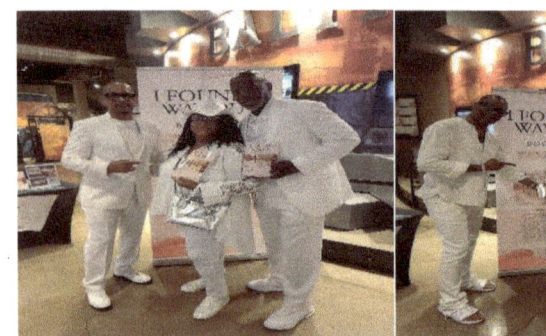

Notes & Sources

Afro American Newspapers/Gado. (1948, November 16). *African American youth playing* Images. https://www.gettyimages.com

Afro American Newspapers/Gado. (1996, August 3). *Building at the Lexington Terrace housing project during demolition by implosion, Baltimore, Maryland. The original caption reads: "Lexington Terrace Public Housing, Al Cc 8/3/96 Blast #1"* [Photograph]. Getty Images. https://www.gettyimages.com

Breslau, N., Davis, G. C., Andreski, P., & Peterson, E. (1991). *Traumatic events and posttraumatic stress disorder in an urban population of young adults.* Archives of General Psychiatry, 48(3), 216–222. https://doi.org/10.1001/archpsyc.1991.01810270028003

Hart, A. Sr. (2025). *I found a way out.* Self-published.

Smith, J. R., & Patton, D. U. (2016). *Posttraumatic stress symptoms in context: Examining trauma responses to violent exposures and homicide death among Black males in urban neighborhoods. American Journal of Orthopsychiatry, 86(2)*, 212–223. https://doi.org/10.1037/ort0000121

Wright, R. (2018, November 28). *Segregated by Design: "Free Choice" and Baltimore Public Housing.* The Metropole. https://themetropole.blog/2018/11/28/segregated-by-design-free-choice-and-baltimore-public-housing/

DON'T CALL ME BACK

Urban Trauma

The journey continues

Author Andre Hart Sr.

A story about overcoming Urban Trauma.

"Don't call me back" isn't rejection.

It's protection. It's clarity. It's love—For the boy Andre once was and the man he became. In his new memoir, *Don't Call Me Back*, Andre picks up where his acclaimed debut, *I Found a Way Out*, left off—not to revisit the pain, but to honor the healing. With poetic urgency and hard-won wisdom, Andre reflects on what it means to set boundaries not from bitterness but from love—for himself, for his past, and for the future he's still building. Raised in a system that punished emotion and labeled him "disruptive" before ever seeing him as a child, Andre's journey was shaped by trauma, defined by resilience, and ultimately transformed by the radical labor of healing. This story is about more than survival.

It's about liberation. About choosing softness without shame. About learning that healing isn't accidental, it's earned. Through grief. Through unlearning. Through walking away from what no longer serves us, even when it hurts. *Don't Call Me Back* is not a story of rejection. It's a story of reclamation. A permission slip to move forward—with intention, with softness, and without apology. A memoir. A boundary. A love letter to becoming. For the ones who grew up too fast. For the ones still learning to feel safe in their own skin.

This story is yours, too.

www.ingramcontent.com/pod-product-compliance
Lightning Source LLC
Chambersburg PA
CBHW051211120626
46547CB00013B/1303